Trauma and Grief

Trauma and Grief

Resources and Strategies for Ministry

R. Scott Sullender

CASCADE *Books* • Eugene, Oregon

TRAUMA AND GRIEF
Resources and Strategies for Ministry

Copyright © 2018 R. Scott Sullender. All rights reserved. Except for brief quotations in critical publications or reviews, no part of this book may be reproduced in any manner without prior written permission from the publisher. Write: Permissions, Wipf and Stock Publishers, 199 W. 8th Ave., Suite 3, Eugene, OR 97401.

Cascade Books
An Imprint of Wipf and Stock Publishers
199 W. 8th Ave., Suite 3
Eugene, OR 97401

www.wipfandstock.com

PAPERBACK ISBN: 978-1-5326-1617-4
HARDCOVER ISBN: 978-1-5326-1619-8
EBOOK ISBN: 978-1-5326-1618-1

Cataloguing-in-Publication data:

Names: Sullender, R. Scott, author.

Title: Trauma and grief : resources and strategies for ministry / R. Scott Sullender.

Description: Eugene, OR: Cascade Books, 2018 | Includes bibliographical references.

Identifiers: ISBN 978-1-5326-1617-4 (paperback) | ISBN 978-1-5326-1619-8 (hardcover) | ISBN 978-1-5326-1618-1 (ebook)

Subjects: LCSH: Psychic trauma—Religious aspects—Christianity. | Bereavement—Religious aspects—Christianity. | Spiritual life—Christianity.

Classification: BT732.7 .S845 2018 (print) | BT732 (ebook)

Manufactured in the U.S.A.   JUNE 15, 2018

Scripture quotations are from New Revised Standard Version Bible, copyright © 1989 National Council of the Churches of Christ in the United States of America. Used by permission. All rights reserved.

Contents

List of Illustrations   vii
Acknowledgments   ix
Introduction   xi

1 Trauma   1
2 Recovery   28
3 Losses   56
4 Grief   80
5 Growth   105
6 Spirituality   121
7 Theological Postscript   146

Appendix 1. Discussion Questions and Activities for Classroom Use   151
Bibliography   159

Illustrations

Figure 1   Impact of Trauma   10
Figure 2   Trauma Grid   13
Figure 3   Trauma and Loss   75
Figure 4   Phases of Grief   83
Figure 5   Faith: Before and After Trauma   129

Acknowledgments

I WANT TO ACKNOWLEDGE first and foremost my social location. I am an older, white, heterosexual male. I am a lifelong Presbyterian, whose members are generally relatively upper-class, well-educated Protestants. I am a licensed psychologist in California with more than forty years of experience in a variety of clinical settings. I think of myself as sensitive to cultural, gender, racial, and ethnic issues. In reading this book, if you come to think otherwise, please accept my apology in advance, and I invite you to drop me an email and share your perspective with me.

I also want to acknowledge that not all of my understanding of trauma and grief comes from my own personal experience and sources such as books and articles. I have also learned a great deal about trauma and grief from my clients, my colleagues, and my students. Among my colleagues, I especially want to thank my friend Herbert Anderson, who read and critiqued a couple of earlier versions of this book. Among the many students I have taught over the last ten years, I want to specifically name the following doctor of ministry students: Ineda Adesanya, Christy Arockiaraj, Janet Bower, Daphyne Brown, Lisa Hebacker, Carole Hyman, Virginia Jackson, Max Lynn, Joanne Martindale, Joyce Parry-Moore, Jeonghyun Park, Jin-Suk Park, Sarai Crain-Pope, Jane Ramsey, Marsha Roth, Kim Stickler, Lois Williams, and Rabbi Joel Zeff. Thanks to each of you for the obvious and not so obvious ways you have been my teacher as well as my student. Finally, a special thanks to the three women in my life, Linda, Lara, and Rebekka, who are unique, delightful, and insightful companions and supporters along my life's journey.

Introduction

LOSSES ARE INEVITABLE. TRAUMA is also nearly inevitable. Nearly a third of all adult Americans will experience at least one major trauma in their lifetime, and that figure does not include the numerous little traumas or the more generalized impact of living in a trauma-oriented media culture. Loss is all around us and impacts us in many ways, both large and small. Trauma is more common than most people realize. Many people go through life harboring unresolved traumas and traumatic losses. They think they are fine or they discount the impact of trauma in their lives. They appear to be functioning well, but unresolved recovery and grief work rob them of their emotional, relational, and spiritual vitality. The dynamics of trauma and grief are found not only on the battlefield and in hospital emergency rooms but permeate the average congregation, too, and congregational caregivers also need to be knowledgeable of and sensitive to the dynamics of trauma and loss.

The traumas and significant losses of people's lives are times of "crisis" in the sense of turning points when they can grow through the experience or decline under the weight of unbearable sorrow and anxiety. How they handle their traumas and significant losses is one of the variables—if not the most important variable—in their overall mental health. Most people respond with some degree of resiliency, but others seemingly never get over it. Similarly, on the relational level, traumas and significant losses are the events that either bind families together in new and powerful ways or leave them scattered and embroiled in conflict. Trauma, particularly traumatic losses, are also the acid tests of faith. Most people turn to religion in times of tragedy and sorrow, but only a few deepen their faith along the way; others are disappointed and turn away from religion. How people handle trauma and significant loss is very important in many different ways.

Introduction

Loss and grief have traditionally been the professional province of the clergy. There is something about the experience of loss and trauma that "brings people to their knees." Traumatized or bereaved people are keenly aware of their helplessness and vulnerability. In most cases, they have been overwhelmed by forces larger than themselves. Trauma and/or traumatic losses prompt them to wrestle with the deeper and "bigger" questions of life and death, questions they might normally put aside in favor of more immediate daily concerns. Thus, in times of trauma and significant loss, many people seek out the services of a clergyperson for wise counsel, for spiritual guidance, and for ritual leadership. Indeed, most Christians naturally seek the services of their pastor or priest, but ministers also report that at times of trauma and loss, they see individuals and families who have not darkened the door of the church in years. As I've already said, there is something about the experience of trauma and loss that brings people to their knees—spiritually, psychologically, and sometimes physiologically and financially. More than any other profession, ministers are expected to provide services to the public in these times and, in essence, to be the experts in loss and grief. So, ministers will do well to understand the dynamics of trauma, loss, and grief, and not just in theoretical terms but also in terms of being able to offer practical skills, tips, and interventions to those who are suffering.

Trauma ministry, ministering to people in the midst of trauma, has long been the province of chaplains—hospital chaplains, military chaplains, police chaplains, fire chaplains, and disaster chaplains. Congregational ministers normally do not encounter as much trauma as chaplains do. Congregational ministers, however, are uniquely and very well equipped to minister to those who are grieving. For centuries, before the advent of modern psychology, ministers were the professional group that served bereaved families. Ministers were the experts in grief. In times of sorrow, people went first to their church or synagogue. In the modern era, ministers have increasingly turned over that job to psychotherapists. The recent focus on the challenges of trauma has only reinforced this transfer of responsibility from ministers to psychotherapists. It is generally assumed by most modern people that therapists are better trained and better equipped than clergy are to help people with loss and trauma. I argue otherwise. First, chaplains have a critical role to play in trauma recovery, and second and most importantly, congregational ministers are still extremely well positioned to help people with their grief work. Ministers and congregations offer five key resources: a supportive community; a set of prescribed and creative rituals; the ability

Introduction

to help people sort out the big questions concerning meaning, purpose, and beliefs; and a basic trust in life's goodness and the human capacity for hope and healing. All of these resources not only help grieving people recover but also, in the language of trauma theory, help people build resiliency. This book addresses all of these resources, but it gives particular attention to the use of rituals in recovery and grief work, which is still one of the distinctive tools of religious caregivers.

This book evolved from graduate-level classes I taught for seminarians. It is based on the lectures and activities I offered my students. If this book is used in the classroom (literal or virtual) or in a clinical training program, I trust that your instructor or supervisor will supplement this book with her or his own material. Each chapter ends with a series of questions for personal reflection that can be used to augment your learning, especially if you are reading this book outside of the classroom context. If you are reading this book as part of a course of study, note that appendix 1 offers group discussion questions and activities for each chapter of the book. I have chosen to keep the footnotes to a minimum. Much of the information that might normally be included in a footnote is incorporated into the questions for reflection at the end of each chapter or in the appendix. I have adopted this format in an effort to not so much write "the last word" on trauma and grief as to provide you, the reader, with a springboard to your continuing learning. May this book be the beginning of your learning, not the end of it.

Trauma, loss, and grief are universal experiences. No one is spared. So, although the primary intended audience of this book is ministers and other spiritual caregivers, it also can be fruitfully read by any spiritually sensitive person in the midst of their own recovery, grief, and growth process. When it comes to loss and trauma, the lines between caregiver and care receiver blur. We are all vulnerable, and we all have occasion to give and receive support; there is a deep, even mystical, connection between giving care and receiving care. This book invites all who have been broken by trauma and loss to read and grow.

Definitions

Trauma and loss are different but overlapping dynamics. Trauma is a blow; loss is a wound. Trauma's primary emotion is fear; loss's primary emotion is grief. Trauma's work is called recovery; loss's work is called healing.

Introduction

This book is primarily about the interface between trauma, loss, and grief. Trauma and loss can stand alone. There are normal *bereavements*, or nontraumatic bereavements, where the primary emotion is grief. There are also *traumas* without bereavement, where the primary emotion is fear. These near-death traumas may appear to not have any significant losses, but it is actually more likely that they have many embedded and unrecognized losses. Finally, there is *traumatic bereavement*, where the primary emotion is traumatic grief, which is a blending of fear and grief. Traumatic bereavement can also be divided into two subcategories: (1) the affected person is involved personally in the trauma and thus witnesses or experiences the death of a loved one(s), colleague(s), or close friend(s), or (2) the affected person is not involved personally in the trauma event and is instead notified of the violent or traumatic death of a loved one, colleague, or close friend. Both of these subcategories involve a mixture of fear and grief but, as one might suppose, the emotional response to the first option leans toward fear, whereas the latter leans toward grief.

In the end, all of the definitions and categories associated with trauma, loss, grief, and growth are not as neat and tidy as scholars might wish. Trauma, bereavement, and traumatic bereavement are not mutually exclusive or even linear. They are overlapping dynamics. In real life, trauma, loss, grief, and even growth are experienced simultaneously and as interwoven, circular dynamics. For purposes of discussion, I will try to tease out the unique features of each, but we should never forget that real life is never as clear as it is in the textbooks.

Pastoral theologians have been writing about loss and grief for years if not centuries, but especially since the advent of modern psychology and its focus on loss and grief as a research interest. My own modest contributions to this literature include *Grief and Growth* (1985) and *Losses in Later Life* (1999). Many other pastoral theologians, pastoral counselors, and Christian counselors have written about loss, grief, and, more recently, trauma. There is much wisdom, lived wisdom, in the Christian community on these important subjects. One of the pieces of wisdom or unique perspectives that Christian and pastoral writers bring to the table is what the late Howard Clinebell called the "growth perspective." How can people grow in and through the otherwise negative experiences of trauma and loss? Another unique piece that theologians bring to the discussion of trauma and grief is their interface with spirituality. Thus, the last two chapters of this volume focus on growth and spirituality.

Introduction

In this book, I use the title "minister" inclusively, covering all of the titles or roles associated with professional religious leadership, such as pastor, minister, priest, chaplain, bishop, elder, superior, and lay pastoral caregiver. Whether you are ordained or not, if you are charged with the spiritual care of one or more Christian believers, please include yourself in this list. This book is for all of you who seek to serve people in times of loss and trauma in the name of Christ.

I am a Christian minister. I write from a broad, ecumenical Christian perspective. I am sure that each of you or your instructors can fill in the specifics related to your denomination or religious tradition. By necessity, I must paint in broad strokes and encourage you to fill in the blanks.

I am sure that my clergy colleagues in Islam, Judaism, and Buddhism could gain much from this volume, but I have chosen to not to try to write from an interfaith perspective. I just do not think I know enough about the fine points of these great religions to do them justice. So I have tried to stick to what I know and write from a broadly Christian perspective. Yet, even within the bounds of this ecumenical approach, there is great diversity of theological assumptions and religious practices. If my ignorance of the particulars of your faith tradition or my theological biases offend you in any way, please forgive me.

Finally, I would like to add a personal note. It is my deepest conviction, based on years of ministry, that in times of loss and trauma, "The Lord is near to the brokenhearted" (Ps 34:18 NRSV). In times of sorrow and tragedy, God takes a step toward us. God seeks to comfort us, to walk with us in our sorrow, to reveal new and deeper truths about God and ourselves, and to sprinkle our lives, even when our eyes are filled with tears, with moments of grace and gratitude. In times of trauma and loss we are more open spiritually than ever . . . and it is also true that God is more available to us than ever. And that is our job, then, as pastoral caregivers, as Christian ministers of all types and kinds—to facilitate that encounter between the living God and the wounded heart. To do our job well, we must be sensitive, wise, and courageous. The work is not easy, but it is very rewarding to witness the birth of new life out of death. And to be a part of people's lives at such moments is indeed an honor and privilege.

R. Scott Sullender
Petaluma, California
www.scottsullender.com

1

Trauma

TRAUMA SEEMS TO BE everywhere these days. Trauma is not new, but it seems to be more obvious, frequent, and intense than ever before. The new term "trauma creep" describes this sense that trauma is everywhere, that the terms "trauma," "traumatic," and "PTSD" are being overused these days, particularly in the news media and social media. Setting aside the overuse of these terms in the media, it is a fair question to raise: Is trauma actually more common these days than ever before? The answer may be a partial "yes." After all, there are more people on planet earth, so the likelihood of a natural disaster impacting population centers is higher than ever before. And climate change is triggering more weather-related disasters than ever before. Terrorism is not new, but technology makes the stakes higher. Terrorists can do more damage than ever before. Are there also more wars, violent crimes, and accidents than ever before? Maybe there is not more in proportion to the population, but the ever-increasing population does lead to more of these traumas. And certainly, as I said at the start, trauma seems to dominate the airwaves, creating a climate of drama and terror.

Trauma has been around since the dawn of human civilization. The Bible contains some vivid examples of trauma, such as the destruction of Jerusalem, the Massacre of the Innocents, and the persecution of early Christians. War has been a source of trauma for centuries. Trauma among soldiers was called "shell shock" in the mid-twentieth century. Post-traumatic stress disorder (PTSD) first received recognition as an identifiable disorder affecting Vietnam veterans in the United States in the 1970s. Americans are also aware that violent crime can be a source of trauma, crimes such as assault and battery, sexual assault, kidnapping, and murder.

Moreover, we have become more aware of the previously hidden traumas caused by domestic violence and child abuse. All of these kinds of traumas are not new in the course of human history, but they do appear to be more common, more visible, these days. Their visibility is a good thing, however, and we do have the media to thank for making us more aware of trauma.

So, given the rising incidence of trauma and the pervasive influence of trauma in our culture, how should ministers and other Christian caregivers be equipped to respond to those suffering from trauma with compassionate and knowledgeable pastoral care? In this first chapter, I touch on the various concepts, issues, and constructs associated with the emerging discipline of trauma studies, noting a few implications for those who minister to people in trauma.

What Is Trauma?

Many different kinds of events and issues are presented to the public as traumatic, so let's define trauma carefully. First, trauma is *a life-threatening event* or series of events. It is an event that is outside of the usual realm of human experience. It is an event that involves people directly in a life-threatening situation. That involvement may be as a victim or even as a witness or first responder. But more than a life-threatening event, which is bad enough, a trauma is also

 a. sudden, unexpected, and unpredictable;
 b. stressful, causing intense fear and subsequent anxiety;
 c. horrific and repulsive to the senses of most people;
 d. overwhelming, rendering people powerless at least momentarily.

Here are some examples:

 a. *Imagine walking into your regular bank and suddenly masked gunmen pull out their guns, shoot into the air, and order everyone down on the floor. It is frightening! You do not know what to expect. Several hostages are crying. The gunmen are shouting orders. One hostage tries to escape and is shot and then pistol whipped. Blood collects on the floor. It makes you sick to your stomach. After five to seven minutes, apparently collecting enough money, the robbers shoot again in the air above the hostages, ordering them not to move, and then flee out of the back door. No one moves. Soon you hear sirens and the police arrive.*

b. *Imagine a Sunday afternoon when you and your family are returning from a weekend visit with relatives. You are driving fifty to sixty miles per hour down the state highway, but suddenly a car in the oncoming lane bangs into another car, pushing the second one across the median barrier into your lane of traffic. You stretch for the brakes, but it happens in a spilt second. You go blank. The last thing you remember is crushing pain to your head and neck. Your car spins around and then rolls, coming to a stop in the ditch. You are semiconscious just long enough to ask if everyone is okay, but no one answers. Then you see an arm severed at the shoulder, dripping blood—whose arm is it? . . . and then you lose consciousness.*

c. *Imagine you are a young mother with four children. Your husband, the father of two of the children, has a terrible drinking problem as well as an anger problem. He has a hard time keeping a job. There is rarely enough food at home. Sometimes, when he is unhappy and has been drinking, he starts berating José, his eight-year-old stepson. You get in between them, and he starts beating you. He throws you against the wall. He breaks your favorite lamp. He screams all kinds of accusations and vulgarities at you and then drives off in the family car. You fear the worst, but the worst part really is that this is not unique. It is almost routine. You think it is not going to happen again, at least that is what he promises, but then it does.*

d. *Imagine living in a small town, surrounded by mountains, with a narrow highway running through it that was the only way in or out. After a week of rain, in the middle of the night, you are wakened by a rumble that grows to a roar. Within seconds, mud and rocks sweep through your yard, burying your garden, barn, and the first floor of your small house. The power goes off. Your children are awake and crying, but they are safe. You are safe. But you fear for your neighbors who live more directly in the path of this avalanche. When morning light arrives, the devastation is clearly horrific. Nothing much is left of your little town, just a sea of mud and debris. After your family is evacuated to a Red Cross center, you help direct rescue workers to the sites of your neighbors' homes. A few survivors are found, but more often, as the hours and days pass, the first responders are pulling corpses from the mud. In total, thirty-seven people die in the avalanche.*

Each of these horrific examples illustrates the essential features of trauma: a life-threatening event or events that is unexpected, creates intense fear, is often horrific or gruesome in nature, and renders participants powerless to control or stop it. That's trauma!

Major Types of Trauma

Generally speaking, trauma events are classified into one of three broad categories based on whether they were caused by a natural disaster, an unintentional human act (i.e., an accident), or an intentional human act.

- Natural disasters include earthquakes, tsunamis, floods, fires, and volcanoes, like the avalanche described in the above vignette.
- Motor vehicle crashes like the one described above are the most common type of accident in the United States, followed by house fires. There are also occasional large-scale transportation accidents, such as train derailments or airplane crashes.
- Violent crime is the major source of intentional human trauma, and it includes muggings, beatings, stabbings, shootings, and rapes. Violent crimes can also occur within intimate relationships and families in the form of spousal battering and child abuse, as described in the above vignette.
- War is another arena in which humans inflict trauma upon one another. Both soldiers and civilians can be victims of trauma by being threatened, by observing, or by being in close proximity to horrific violence and destruction. Torture and human slavery are other examples of prolonged human-caused traumas.

The distinctions between these three categories of trauma are not always clear but are surprisingly important to people. Was hurricane Katrina really a natural disaster or was it a human-caused disaster? Is a particular airplane crash an accident or a terrorist act or the result of human error? Much of the news reporting around trauma events is focused on determining which category a particular trauma belongs in. This debate is not just a theoretical discussion. There are certain legal implications, but the issue also affects the recovery process of the survivors. Generally speaking, the recovery process for people caught in trauma's wake is easier if the trauma is understood to be a natural disaster or an accident rather than an intentional act by another person.

How many Americans experience trauma? It is difficult to generalize about all Americans because exposure to trauma varies according to living environment and each individual's psychosocial history. However, surveys of the general population often estimate that about one-half of Americans have experienced or will experience a major trauma in their lifetime.[1] Maybe trauma is more common than we might realize. There are a myriad of ways that people can be traumatized.

Trauma Spectrum

Robert Scaer, in his book *The Trauma Spectrum*, argues that trauma is best understood as on a continuum.[2] There are full-scale traumas and there are "little traumas." The latter are "little" in the sense that not all four of the essential defining features of a trauma noted above are operative. A trauma may be unexpected but not horrific. It may be life-threatening but not overwhelming. And so on. Or, a "little" trauma could have elements of all four features but at a relatively mild level of intensity. Among these hidden, unrecognized little traumas are many medical procedures, which, Scaer suggests, are more traumatic than most physicians or patients realize.[3] Chief among medical procedures that need to be understood in a trauma framework are the procedures and treatments associated with cancer. Cancer treatment can be traumatic on many levels. First, the word *cancer* can itself be terrifying and rather overwhelming. Second, the language of warfare that surrounds cancer treatment can be upsetting, making patients feel that they are powerless and that their bodies are the collateral damage in a larger, epic struggle. Then, there are the actual procedures, the major surgeries or chemotherapy treatments that are traumatic to the body as well as the psyche.

"Little traumas" may actually be an oxymoron. Trauma is by definition something big, something out of the ordinary. Many events might be traumatic but not a trauma event. This is reflected in the distinction between "trauma," the noun, and "traumatic," the adjective. The concept of trauma

1. Briere and Scott, *Principles of Trauma Therapy*, 4.
2. Scaer, *Trauma Spectrum*, 2.
3. Scaer, *Trauma Spectrum*, 151–73.

as being on a spectrum might contribute to what was earlier called trauma creep, the increasing use of the word *trauma* to describe experiences that do not meet the full criteria of the concept. Nevertheless, Scaer's point is noted, and I will come back to it again in this book; trauma is more common than we might realize, and thus its impact is not always recognized. Another corollary of this insight is that trauma is both an objective reality and a subjective perception.

A Single Event vs. a Prolonged Trauma

Some traumas are single events. Other traumas are a series of events or a continuous "event" or situation. The traditional definition of trauma is that it is an event or a series of events. Some scholars, notably Judith Herman in her 1992 classic *Trauma and Recovery*, have also drawn the world's attention to situations of prolonged trauma, such as being tortured or being a victim of domestic violence or being repeatedly abused as a child. Herman argues that these situations merit inclusion in the definition of trauma. Moreover, she also argues that the prolonged nature of such traumas, which she likens to captivity, create a different set of symptoms and treatment problems than do single-event traumas. She proposed a new diagnosis, complex post-traumatic stress disorder, to describe the unique set of symptoms created by chronic trauma.[4] Indeed, prolonged trauma seems to create a set of symptoms that are themselves chronic, including helplessness, paralysis, and depression. Herman's book created a stir. Could chronic situations also be considered a type of trauma? Some have said "no"—that trauma has to be an event and, in particular, an unexpected event. The unexpected or surprise nature of trauma is an essential defining feature of trauma. Others have said "yes"—that situations such as chronic child abuse, domestic violence, extended torture, or capture must be considered a type of trauma and that their impact on people should be viewed through the lens of PTSD. In the end, the fifth edition (2013) of the *Diagnostic and Statistical Manual of Mental Disorders* (*DSM-5*) does not officially recognize complex PTSD as a new diagnosis, but it does recognize prolonged trauma as a type of trauma capable of leading to PTSD.

While focusing on trauma's duration, it should be noted that the longer a person is exposed to trauma, the more severe his or her resulting

---

4. Herman, *Trauma and Recovery*. See especially chapter 6.

trauma symptoms. This principle applies to whatever length of exposure is being considered, whether the exposure was ten minutes, an hour, a day, a week, or even years. Generally speaking, the longer one is exposed to trauma, the greater the impact and potential harm. This is why people who are trapped in prolonged traumas, such as people who have been imprisoned and tortured, kidnapped and enslaved, or involved in an intimate relationship characterized by violence and fear, have higher rates of PTSD than those exposed to single-event traumas. Other variables are at work, of course, such as the degree of threat, the resiliency of the individuals, and the availability of support services, but, generally speaking, the longer people are exposed to trauma, the more severe the symptoms.

Developmental Trauma

It is also true that the younger a person is when she or he is exposed to trauma, particularly a prolonged trauma, the more damaging the impact. Traumas that children experience are now being labeled as "developmental traumas," traumas that damage the psychosocial development of children. These traumas are typically prolonged, life-threatening situations that are chronic or are a series of traumatic events. Developmental traumas are usually interpersonal in nature, meaning they are traumas caused intentionally by a trusted family member or friend. In *The Body Keeps the Score*, psychiatrist Bessel van der Kolk argues that these traumas are "a hidden epidemic" in American society.[5] He goes on to argue that the diagnosis of PTSD, which largely applies to adults and single-event traumas, does not adequately describe the complexities and unique set of symptoms, such as self-mutilation, associated with childhood trauma.

The research that supports this view includes the recently published Adverse Childhood Experiences Study (or the ACE Study), co-funded by the Centers for Disease Control and Kaiser Permanente of San Diego, California. This study revealed the long-term and largely unconscious impact of childhood trauma.[6] From 1995 to 1997, the study surveyed 17,000 Kaiser patients using a simple questionnaire consisting of ten items. The content of each item, however, was neither simple nor lightweight. Each question addressed a major childhood adverse event or situation such as

5. van der Kolk, *The Body Keeps the Score*, 151.
6. "Adverse Childhood Experiences," *Centers for Disease Control and Prevention*, http://www.cdc.gov/violenceprevention/acestudy/.

sexual abuse, neglect, alcoholic parent, or domestic violence. The results noted a striking link between the degree of childhood adverse events and adult diseases and adult psychological and social problems. Adults with higher ACE scores were at risk for health problems such as obesity and heart disease and various social problems such as imprisonment, addictions, suicide, and marital instability. This study also revealed that trauma is more common in childhood than most people had realized.

The reasons why childhood trauma is so damaging should be obvious. First, the trauma is usually chronic, thus intensifying its impact. Second, children and teens are more vulnerable to the damaging effects of prolonged trauma because their brains are still forming. If they live in a chronic state of alarm and arousal, this condition becomes woven into their mental and neurological wiring. Further, they have not yet acquired the coping skills, including the verbal skills, for understanding and processing their emotions related to trauma. Finally, children and teens often do not have the social or family support to cope successfully with trauma, especially not, of course, if the source of the trauma is a trusted family member.

Collective Trauma

In addition to individual traumas, there are also collective traumas. Like individual traumas, collective traumas are life-threatening events that are unpredictable, stressful, horrific, and overwhelming, at least for a few moments. The difference is that collective traumas impact large numbers of people. Natural disasters are almost always collective traumas. Natural disasters strike random groups of people, with or without a common identity. They tend to forge community and even a new temporary identity as victims or survivors. In contrast to natural disasters, collective traumas that are human-caused and deliberate are usually aimed at particular groups of people with a common preexisting identity, such as Jews, Muslims, or African Americans.[7] Such acts of terror strike at the group as a whole, at its collective identity and sometimes at its very existence as a collectivity. If the trauma is repetitive and transcends generations, the term "cultural trauma" (coined by Jeff Alexander) may be used to describe the systematic

---

7. Some religious or denominational groups are born in trauma, particularly in the form of persecution. Trauma then comes to shape their identity, values, and beliefs.

destruction of a group's culture.[8] But even single-event collective traumas may shape or reshape a group's social identity. If that is the case, then it is not hard to imagine that this altered identity is passed down to succeeding generations as what is now commonly called "generational trauma," thus extending the trauma's impact through the years.

For most Americans, the most striking and powerful collective trauma in recent memory is the terror attacks on that took place on September 11, 2001. For most people, it was a shock; it was life-threatening, it was horrific, and it was emotionally overwhelming. Significantly, most people were exposed to this trauma not directly but indirectly through the electronic media. The electronic media extended the trauma's impact and strengthened people's sense of shared tragedy. Collective traumas are, by definition, shared tragedies. People suffer together. They have been attacked or threatened not individually but as a people, even as a nation. As a collective trauma, 9/11 amped up Americans' collective anxiety, shook up our national identity, challenged our cherished values, and altered our common history.

All collective traumas, whether natural or human-caused, create varying degrees of stress or trauma symptoms in individuals based on the proximity of those individuals to the trauma's epicenter. The degree of impact is usually presented graphically as concentric circles drawn to represent the degree of emotional or physical proximity to "ground zero." People in the innermost circle are impacted the most and often are most at risk for negative consequences. In the widening outer circles, many more people experience the same trauma but at reduced levels of intensity. Sometimes, this graphic of concentric circles is used to represent the primary, secondary, and tertiary impact of trauma (see figure 1).

---

8. Alexander, *Trauma*, 6.

Figure 1
Impact of Trauma

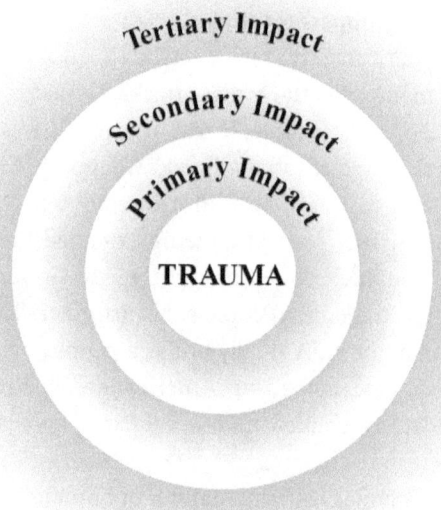

Primary impact refers to those people at the site of a trauma who are impacted directly and personally. *Secondary* refers to those people who were not at the site of the trauma but who know people who were there and were impacted (injured or died) and thus are impacted indirectly but still personally. This is a larger number of people than those who are directly impacted. *Tertiary* refers to those people who were not at the site of the trauma, nor do they know anyone affected, but they are impacted through media exposure. This circle is the largest number of people.

Collective traumas are not experienced the same by everyone. Within each trauma, there are subgroups and people at various distances, emotionally and physically, from the trauma. The same distinctions or drawing of concentric circles could be applied to smaller social units, such as families or congregations. The degree of impact of a trauma upon a particular individual depends in part on their relative emotional and physical distance from the trauma. In short, traumas are not monoliths. Everyone's experience of a common trauma is unique. Or, to put this in the language of narrative, the community has a story, and there are individual stories within the larger story. We can understand the trauma on a collective level, seeing the big picture, and also experience it on an individual level, "up front and personal."

Notification of a Traumatic Death

Congregational ministers encounter traumatic losses from time to time, but ministers who serve as military chaplains, hospital chaplains, police chaplains, fire chaplains, or disaster chaplains deal with traumatic death regularly. Violent losses are the daily fare in the emergency rooms of most hospitals, among the families of military personnel, among prisoners, and among disturbed and troubled youth. Ministers are often called upon to accompany other professionals when the next of kin must be notified of a loved one's traumatic, unexpected, and violent death. Many examples come to mind:

- Military chaplains often accompany other officers when they visit the family of a fallen soldier bearing the news of his or her death.
- Hospital chaplains are often invited to accompany medical professionals in the emergency room of hospitals to tell the arriving family that their loved one just died in a car accident or was murdered.
- A volunteer police chaplain may be asked to accompany police officers when they go to the home of a family to notify them that their loved one died a violent death.
- In the aftermath of a natural disaster, ministers may be asked to accompany people when they visit the morgue to identify the body of a loved one.

These are emotionally intense situations. They are particularly challenging if the chaplain does not know the family. They walk into the room blind, so to speak, not knowing what to expect. Yet, their high calling is to handle this task as compassionately and professionally as possible so that the act of notification does not itself become a secondary trauma and its adverse effects are minimized. Ministers are invited to be present because they are skilled at stabilizing and comforting people in crisis. May it be so!

When ministers or chaplains are involved in the notifying of next of kin of the traumatic death of a loved one, here are a few simple principles that they follow (five words that begin with P):

- Find a *private* place where the news can be given and received, out of the public eye, with respect for the import of the moment and respect for the privacy of the family.

- Be *prepared* for strong emotions. Have a steady, firm, and calm manner. Speak with directness and compassion. Be an available and ready container for strong emotions.

- Be *present* in the moment as much as possible, non-anxiously. Be compassionate and yet direct in communications, willing to sit with family members' pain, sorrow, and unanswered questions.

- Be *patient*. It takes time to sit with a family while they process horrible news. It takes time and patience.

- Be a good *provider*. Provide information about the kinds of symptoms a traumatized person or family might experience in the first few days and nights ahead. Giving good information is important. It helps the family and friends to not be unduly frightened or overwhelmed. This information needs to be provided in both written and verbal form because people in shock do not remember much of what anyone says. Follow up with the family the next day or a few days later. When necessary, provide referrals and follow-up support.

Ministering to people who are in the midst of trauma is intense work. It is also risky work. Traumatic grief can easily become complicated grief, grief with medical complications, or prolonged grief. Traumatic grief is more likely to require professional assistance because the grief is overlaid with trauma recovery work. Competent and mature spiritual care is critical to a successful passage through traumatic losses.

Trauma's Impact

Trauma's impact depends on several variables. I have already mentioned four: length of exposure, proximity to trauma, age of the victim, and how comprehensive the trauma is. These variables and others are represented graphically in figure 2.

Figure 2
Trauma Grid

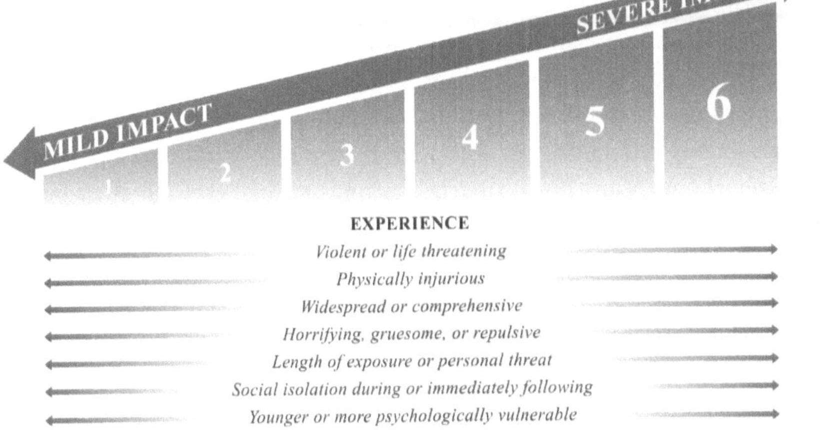

MILD IMPACT → 1 2 3 4 5 6 ← **SEVERE IMPACT**

EXPERIENCE

- Violent or life threatening
- Physically injurious
- Widespread or comprehensive
- Horrifying, gruesome, or repulsive
- Length of exposure or personal threat
- Social isolation during or immediately following
- Younger or more psychologically vulnerable

The trauma grid is a helpful tool for caregivers to keep in mind when ministering to a trauma victim. It provides a framework for quickly assessing the likely degree of impact and severity of symptoms of the trauma.

Traumatic Stress

Trauma is by definition stressful because it is, by its very nature, overwhelming stress, stress that immobilizes people and impacts them in various conscious and unconscious ways. The damage traumatic stress does is multidimensional, but it is particularly insidious in terms of human health.

In the last fifty years or so, stress has been extensively studied. Physicians know that a person's body reacts via the autonomic nervous system to any perceived stressor. When our brain perceives a threat, it automatically (without conscious awareness) initiates certain changes in our physiological and chemical functioning. Blood pressure goes up; sugar is released into the blood for quick energy; and the heart pumps faster, muscle tension increases, and adrenaline pours into the bloodstream. The brain also shuts down any nonessential body functions such as digestion for the duration of the threat.[9] All of these changes serve to equip us for action so that we can "fight or flee" the perceived danger. In previous eons, these reactions were successful in helping humans survive the many threats from their

---

9. Later, I argue that the stress or threat response also shuts down nonessential emotional processing, such as grief work.

environment. And, these changes worked. In a sense, humans are built for trauma. Through the fight-or-flight syndrome, we mobilize for action in the heat of the moment.

For modern people living in industrialized and large metropolitan areas, stress is not so much short-lived as it is chronic. Modern stress is more often prolonged and drawn out, such as the threat people feel from living in an abusive relationship or a constantly demanding job or a high-crime neighborhood. Many people live in a chronic state of arousal. Their blood pressure and adrenaline levels are chronically high, and their muscles are chronically tense. This is a dilemma modern people find themselves in when it comes to stress. What was designed as a short-lived crisis response has become a semipermanent reality. What was designed for trauma has become chronic.

Physicians and medical professionals report that stress, especially prolonged stress, is damaging to human health. Chronic stress is a risk factor for hypertension and thus heart disease and stroke. Even conditions that we might not think of as induced by stress, such as the onset of cancer, seem to be affected by chronic stress. This is so because stress impacts the human immune system, lowering resistance to disease. Even ordinary illnesses such as influenza are more common in people living with chronic stress. Chronic stress is also a risk factor for mental illness, family instability, and general unhappiness in life. Chronic stress brings on many health risks. All of this is well documented. The role of chronic stress in health is one of the great discoveries of the last sixty years of medical science.

Trauma events are stressful events. The stress may initially be sudden, intense, and short-lived, but it may become chronic and prolonged if a person's exposure to threat is continuous or repetitive. Either way, it impacts our bodies in ways that most people are generally not aware of. We often do not realize the toll stress takes on our bodies. We get used to chronic stress. It becomes "the new normal," as crazy as that sounds. Even after our minds and emotions have calmed down, our bodies can harbor the lingering effects of traumatic stress.

Traumatic stress is unique precisely because it can be very overwhelming, sudden, and intense. This type of stress has been the subject of a number of specialized studies. Sometimes people make the analogy that the human nervous system is like the electrical wiring of one's home. When something traumatic happens, the stress overwhelms our nervous system, blowing the fuses or triggering the breakers of our nervous system. This metaphor is reflected in the familiar phrase "a nervous breakdown." This is an apt analogy for mild or moderate forms of trauma and traumatic stress, but what happens in severe trauma is that the stress is so intense that the circuits do not just shut down, they are "fried"—the wiring itself is burned up. This is traumatic stress! It overwhelms the autonomic nervous system entirely, immobilizing people rather than arousing them to fight or flight. Scholars now say that in such circumstances humans move into a "freeze" reaction. Unable to fight or flee, people become passive, much like a deer in a car's headlights. The freeze response is a last-ditch effort to ward off imminent death. Sometimes it works. Sometimes the perpetrator, if the trauma is human-caused, loses interest and spares our lives. But what happens when the trauma is chronic? What happens to humans in circumstances of prolonged trauma, such as being imprisoned and tortured repeatedly for years or being abused sexually by a perpetrator for years and years? Indeed, in these cases fight or flight does not work. Maybe the Stockholm syndrome response (capture bonding) does not work either. The only response is a physiological freeze. Over time, the freeze morphs into passivity, chronic depression, and learned helplessness. People give up. It is futile to resist, to fight, or to flee. Traumatic stress is insidious in this way.

Trauma Symptoms

Traumatic stress, especially during the first month after a trauma, is not a disorder; it is not a sign of mental illness. It is quite normal to be traumatized by a trauma! Trauma responses are normal reactions to abnormal events. What is "abnormal" is not the people or their reactions but the event. It is common to experience somatic distress such as headache, upset stomach, muscle tension, and insomnia in the immediate aftermath of a trauma event. Mentally, this short-term, intense stress leads to distressing dreams, flashbacks, restlessness, emotional numbing, and perhaps irritability. People involved in a trauma need to expect these kinds of reactions and to be encouraged in the days or weeks following a trauma to take measures to mitigate these symptoms.

Psychological reactions to trauma are generally clustered into three areas, as follows.

Excessive Excitability and Arousal

One of the essential features of all traumas is that it is a life-threatening situation that provokes intense fear. So, it is understandable that this intense fear carries over, that it continues for hours, days, or weeks after the trauma event in the form of anxiety. After a trauma event or a release from a prolonged trauma situation, most people need some time to calm down. Cortisol levels tend to decline slowly. Their nervous system has been traumatized, overly aroused and stimulated. They may still be on edge, hypervigilant, anticipating the next disaster. They may be easily frightened or startled and "jump out of their skins" if surprised. They feel guarded and vulnerable and scan the environment for the next threat. As a soldier once said, it is as if they are on "permanent alert status." This kind of intense anxiety makes it difficult to relax and difficult to sleep, even apart from the negative effect of bad dreams or nightmares. It may also make it difficult to concentrate or remember much. It may make people more irritable—more prone to outbursts of anger, blaming, or even rage. Within the family context, this kind of intense anxiety leads to efforts to control or overprotect loved ones.

Numbed Withdrawal and Avoidance

Some traumas are so overwhelming, so gruesome, and so painful that people become numb emotionally in the midst of the trauma, which I referred to earlier as the freeze response. They shut down because that is the safest and best way to handle the overwhelming flood of stimuli and threat. This reaction can be experienced as psychic numbing, emotional anesthesia, or a trance-like state. This emotional shutting down is meant to be a temporary measure or an emergency response. Normally, people start to feel again as the threat dissipates, but for some people this emotional numbing lingers. What was normal at the time of the trauma becomes maladaptive days, weeks, or months later.

Numbing turns into avoiding. People try to avoid all reminders of the trauma, which might include even seemingly unconnected things. They do this by refusing to talk about it. They do this by avoiding people, places, or keepsakes that remind them of the trauma. They are frightened, frightened of experiencing that threat, that terror, that horror again . . . and so they avoid. This desire to numb out and avoid is reinforced by the overuse of alcohol or drugs. Typically, traumatized persons increase their consumption of alcohol and use of drugs and perform other addictive behaviors, all of which largely work in the short run. Intoxicated people do not feel much; their senses are numbed and their feelings and memories dulled. Alcohol works, for a time.

This emotional numbing and avoiding can lead to a withdrawal from life's activities, what Judith Herman calls "a constriction of life."[10] Along with emotional anesthesia comes a general withdrawal from life's activities and social engagement with friends and family. Traumatized persons often become cut off from others, isolated and disconnected. This is especially the case if the trauma was caused by another human being. Women who have been raped, for example, might avoid sexual intimacy, even with someone they normally trust. Wives might describe their traumatized husband as cut off, walled off, or emotionally detached—certainly a different person than before the trauma. They might be passive, just sitting and staring for periods. Suppressing or avoiding painful feelings or memories is a costly defense mechanism because all human emotions are linked together. Normally, people cannot avoid or suppress one feeling in isolation from all other feelings. So, joy and love go away, along with threat and anxiety. And life becomes constricted, at least for a time.

Repetitive, Intrusive Memories or Recollections

People who have been traumatized may be unable to remember significant portions or the details of the trauma event. Some people may even have partial or full amnesia when it comes to the trauma. Their memories of what happened are not truly forgotten, just lodged in the unconscious mind. Such memories are too overwhelming and painful to remember, much less talk about. One of the ways that the mind tries to reintegrate these painful memories is through dreams. Traumatized people typically have intense dreams in the aftermath of a trauma. Some dreams are pretty literal, a reenactment of the trauma, and may result in the dreamer waking up in a sweat or even in terror. Other dreams are more symbolic or indirect, dreams in which the dreamer is trapped, caught by surprise, or abandoned. Remembering and talking through one's dreams is a good way to reintegrate memories into one's conscious mind.

---

10. See Herman, *Trauma and Recovery*, 42–47.

Dissociation

Traumatized people dissociate to one degree or another, depending on how overwhelming the trauma experience was. However, walled-off memories do not stay walled off. In time, people generally start to remember, to fill in the blanks of what happened. They can be assisted to recall what happened by talking to other victims, first responders, or eyewitnesses. Remembering what happened is part of the recovery process.

People who have been through more severe or prolonged traumas may have more intense and more rigidly walled-off memories. In such cases, flashbacks or fragments of their trauma memories will break through into their consciousness like "flash bulbs" during waking hours, leading to an instant or even a few minutes when they feel that they are actually back at the trauma event again. These flashback memories are often partial, highly visual, and emotionally charged. To the untrained observer, it looks as if the trauma survivor blacks out for an instant or "leaves the room." These intrusive recollections, especially the flashbacks, are often triggered by a particular sight, sound, smell, or strong emotion. Similar stressful events might also trigger memories. These involuntary recollections can be frightening. People can easily conclude that they are going crazy. Instead, such activity should be understood as the mind's attempts, however frightening, to come to terms with what happened. If carefully managed, and with professional support, most people can fully remember what happened. In rare cases, trauma memories can remain walled off for years and only resurface years later as "recovered memories."

There is another aspect of the dynamics of dissociation that bears some comment. If the trauma involves physical pain, bodily injury, or abuse of the body, people may dissociate from their bodies, from their bodily sensations. They might experience what some call an out-of-body experience. They disconnect from their own bodily senses and their experience of their surroundings. This aspect of dissociation, like dissociation in general, is a survival mechanism, albeit a desperate and costly one. This type of bodily disconnect can continue for days, weeks, or months after the trauma has passed. Thus, an important part of the trauma recovery process must be efforts to reconnect with one's body, to experience sensations again but this time not be overwhelmed by them. This work may be complicated when the trauma resulted in injuries and physical damage to the body. Healing can take some time. Restoration and strengthening of one's body will speed the psychological aspects of recovery.

TRAUMA

Post-Traumatic Stress Disorder (PTSD)

Most people recover from trauma. Within a few days or a few weeks, most experience a reduction in their trauma symptoms. Some people do not recover or do not recover fully or easily. If a person's symptoms continue into the second and third months following a trauma event or the release from a trauma situation, and if the symptoms are causing significant distress and impairment, the person needs to be evaluated by a professional. They may merit the diagnosis of post-traumatic stress disorder and need professional assistance to fully recover. Not everyone who is traumatized ends up with PTSD. Only 8 to 12 percent of people who are exposed to a trauma are diagnosed with PTSD, although the rate of PTSD increases to 30 to 40 percent for victims recovering from rape or torture.[11] Obviously, some traumas have stronger impacts than others, and some people are more vulnerable to getting PTSD than other people. Nevertheless, it should be emphasized that PTSD is not a mental illness per se. I like to think of PTSD as a failure of the recovering process or as a resiliency disorder.

As noted earlier, the autonomic nervous system controls the body's internal organs. It operates automatically, without conscious thought. The primary area of the brain that controls this system is the hypothalamus. The autonomic nervous system is divided into two branches: the sympathetic nervous system and the parasympathetic nervous system. Under threat of danger, the sympathetic nervous system quickly activates the body for action. When the threat has passed, the parasympathetic nervous system dampens the body's alarm mechanisms, returning the body to rest mode. One way of understanding PTSD is to think of these two systems as damaged. Indeed, the hypothalamic-pituitary-adrenal axis *is* damaged in PTSD patients. As a result, the parasympathetic nervous system cannot do its job. It cannot recover. In other words, PTSD is a failure of recovery at the neurological level.

When a person's head receives a violent, unexpected blow, the resulting damage may be diagnosed as *traumatic brain disorder*. Traumatic brain disorders have received media attention in recent years. Concussions are one example of traumatic brain disorder. War injuries, such as when a soldier's brain is damaged by an explosion or by gunfire, is another example. Transportation crashes are another source of traumatic brain injuries. Traumatic brain disorder is the physical, or neurological, version of PTSD.

---

11. American Psychiatric Association, *DSM-5*, 276.

People diagnosed with a traumatic brain disorder are more likely to also be diagnosed with PTSD. Post-traumatic stress disorder and traumatic brain disorder overlap. Post-traumatic stress disorder includes and assumes certain neurological damage, and people with traumatic brain disorder have certain predictable psychological symptoms. Physical healing and trauma recovery go hand in hand.

Trapped in Time

Shelly Rambo, in her book *Spirit and Trauma: A Theology of Remaining*, posits: "Trauma is the suffering that does not go away. The study of trauma is the study of what remains."[12] Later, she notes that trauma throws the adage "time heals all wounds" on its head. Trauma distorts time. I would prefer to say that the dynamics of PTSD distort time or keep its victims "trapped in time." When people suffering from PTSD have a flashback, it is as if they are back there again, back at the trauma event(s), reliving the horror. They may relive the trauma for only a few seconds or perhaps a few minutes, but for those few seconds or minutes, it is real. Their body reacts as if they are there again, under threat. It is all very real! And in those few seconds or minutes, traumatized people are not in the present, in the here and now. Loved ones will say that they "checked out" or were in a brief trance. In those few minutes, the trauma pulls them back into the past, to the "there and then." Flashbacks, dreams, and other intrusive thoughts are the most dramatic examples of this dynamic. In the words of Rambo, the trauma remains. It lingers long after the event is over and people are safe. In a sense, PTSD might be understood as a type of time warp!

In a more generalized way, people with chronic PTSD can also be understood as bound by the past. They have come to define their lives, their identity, and even their very souls by something horrible that happened years if not decades earlier. Again, using the imagery introduced by Rambo, people with PTSD are stuck in Holy Saturday: the trauma event of Good Friday is over, but the new life of Easter has yet to emerge. People with chronic PTSD are permanently "in the middle." Post-traumatic stress disorder might be understood as a problem with time, as the result of a damaged portion of the brain that regulates time, preventing some traumatized persons from coming fully into the present, much less embracing a new future. PTSD is a failure to come into the present.

12. Rambo, *Spirit and Trauma*, 15.

Post-Traumatic Rape Syndrome

As noted earlier, several traumas are deemed so unique that their impact bears special consideration. Two examples, complex PTSD (prolonged trauma) and developmental trauma disorder (childhood trauma), have already been discussed. These subtypes of PTSD have symptoms in common with PTSD and also have some symptoms that are unique to the specific type of trauma. Professionals who work with victims of sexual violence—and there are many types and degrees of sexual violence, too—have attempted to describe the unique impact of the trauma of rape. The most common formulation is referred to as either rape trauma syndrome[13] or as post-traumatic rape syndrome. Rape trauma syndrome is understood to be similar to, but distinct from, PTSD. Several PTSD symptoms, such as initial emotional numbing, intense anxiety and fear, intrusive thoughts, dissociation, and loss of memory can present in a typical rape victim. In addition, victims of sexual assault have to bear the burden of shame, being threatened or pressured into silence, and/or told in overt and subtle ways that the rape was their fault. People recovering from sexual assault are also more likely to struggle with self-loathing, reenactment behaviors, self-mutilation, and depression compared to those with a more generalized PTSD. As a result, victims of sexual assault often need specialized treatment and recovery programs that address their unique experience and symptoms.

Retraumatization

People who are in the early stages of trauma recovery can be retraumatized if they are placed into a situation (emotional, interpersonal, or physical) that is similar to their original trauma. The new or similar situation triggers or intensifies trauma symptoms. In the case of an earthquake, for example, aftershocks can trigger renewed anxieties. Or, consider a soldier who is deployed on another tour of duty in the war zone before he or she has recovered from the trauma associated with the first exposure. Sometimes forcing people to talk about or relive their trauma before they feel safe and emotionally stable can result in retraumatization. Another often cited and

---

13. Psychiatrist Ann Wolbert Burgess and sociologist Lynda Lytle Holmstrom coined the term "rape trauma syndrome" in 1974 while working at Boston City Hospital. See Burgess and Holmstrom, "Rape Trauma Syndrome." The definition of the syndrome has been reviewed and revised over the years. Burgess has since written several helpful books on rape and recovery.

all too common example is the female rape victim who is forced to tell her story to law enforcement authorities again and again and then tell it still again under the cross-examination of an adversarial, verbally abusive attorney. All of this can be quite retraumatizing rather than empowering if the individual is not given adequate social support and emotional tools.

Returning to the metaphor of the household electrical system, severely traumatized people have wiring that is so damaged that their nervous systems cannot hold even a normal electrical load. They cannot simply flip the circuit breaker back on and expect everything to be fine. Their wiring has been fried, so to speak. Until that wiring is restored or repaired, they are vulnerable to another electrical overload. Signs of that vulnerability include hypersensitivity to stress, to perceived threats, and to surprises, as well as overreacting to similar events or even reliving the initial trauma in the form of repeated storytelling. Trauma impacts the body, and the body remembers.

Retraumatization is a very important topic for caregivers. If trauma is involved, caregivers must resist the temptation to rush in and "make someone talk it out." Trauma victims might not be ready or able to talk about it until other tasks are accomplished first, such as making sure they are safe, their medical condition is stabilized, and they are receiving adequate social support. Yet, each person is different. Each trauma has a different impact. People dealing with the immediate aftermath of a natural disaster can probably benefit from talking it through fairly quickly, but people recently released from a prolonged period of torture need to be stabilized and learn to manage their anxiety first. Caregivers must assess each situation carefully. In this regard, it is important to note, as I will throughout this book, that trauma recovery is not the same as grief work. Yes, there is overlap. Good trauma recovery should eventually lead to and include grief work, but trauma recovery work must begin by directly addressing the PTSD symptoms.

Reenactment

Mental health professionals who specialize in treating people with PTSD suggest that some traumatized people unconsciously reenact their trauma in certain ways. An example of this concept might be a person who was sexually abused as a child and now acts out sexually as a teen or adult in ways similar to his or her earlier abuse. Another example might be a veteran who engages in dangerous or risky behavior as a way of unconsciously trying to redo his or her wartime trauma. These "reenactments" are seen as unconscious attempts to redo the trauma. The "redos" may be attempts to master what was initially overwhelming, an exercise in self-punishment, or just a way to come to terms with what happened. Unfortunately, reenactments rarely work and can be quite self-destructive. If caregivers observe reenactment behaviors in someone with PTSD, they need to consult with a mental health professional.

Vicarious Traumatization

In more recent decades, as trauma studies have multiplied, another concept has surfaced among the therapeutic professions. This concept is vicarious traumatization. When psychotherapists work closely with traumatized persons, they start to experience, in milder forms, the same trauma symptoms as their patients. In other words, they experience higher levels of anxiety, anger, sleep difficulties, and distorted memory. Those who work with female rape victims report that they can even come to mirror their patients' worldview, namely, disgust with men. This dynamic is not limited to therapists. Spouses of returning soldiers also report this dynamic.

Human emotions are contagious. Laughter is infectious. Weeping tends to invoke sadness and even tears in others. In the case of trauma, the primary emotional contagion is fear or anxiety. Hearing and experiencing another's fear is upsetting and tends to activate similar emotions in caregivers. In the midst of trauma, fear's infectious nature creates panic. In the aftermath of a trauma, the fear and anxiety that haunt trauma victims are still contagious. The transference of emotional material from one person to another depends in part on the intensity of the emotions, and trauma-related emotions are intense, and in part on the intimacy of the relationship. It might also have something to do with how certain people are wired. Research from neuroscience suggests that humans have certain types of brain cells in their frontal lobes, called mirror neurons, that give them the capacity to literally be in sync with one another. These mirror neurons have their origins in the early attunement between mother and infant. They facilitate our capacity to imitate others and thereby learn from observation and imitation. The mirror neurons are mostly in the frontal area of the brain and constitute only 10 percent of the neurons in the brain. Even so, they help us feel what another feels. In other words, empathy is not just an emotional thing; empathy occurs even on a cellular level. The dynamics of empathy are that strong! No wonder empathy is so healing. At the same time, because caregivers who work closely and consistently with traumatized people are vulnerable to trauma symptoms themselves, regular supervision and self-care are essential components of trauma-based ministries.

Strategies for Caregiving

In this chapter, I have briefly surveyed the various constructs, issues, and dynamics of trauma as they are emerging in the literature and among trauma therapists. I have thrown a lot at you, the reader, in a short space! I hope you will follow up with the personal reflections, classroom activities, and recommended readings. But, for the moment, I offer three important takeaways for ministers and other spiritual caregivers.

First, traumas vary widely in kind and degree. Trauma or traumatic experiences are more common than a minister or a congregation might imagine. People often do not recognize a given experience as a trauma event because it is not obviously a trauma or because it is private or is stigmatized. Caregivers can help greatly simply by naming an event or experience as a trauma or traumatic, thus giving people permission to take their experience seriously. In order to name it, caregivers need to be familiar with the variations of trauma discussed in this chapter. Second, ministers can help by understanding people's various physiological, psychological, and social problems as possible trauma symptoms. For example, a believer's overreaction to a seemingly ordinary event might be a sign of retraumatization. Identifying it as such might help normalize it and give the believer permission to "be kind to themselves" and, if appropriate, get professional assistance. Third, talking with traumatized people is upsetting. Their stories can be horrifying. Their anxiety and fears are infectious. Like most people, ministers and caregivers may prefer to avoid the subject altogether and/or discount the significance of what appears to be an overly dramatic and needy parishioner. Rather, ministers can be more helpful by engaging with traumatized people and taking their suffering seriously. Finally, ministers can do all of the above tasks by lifting up before God and one another the event and/or a person's experience in rituals. Rituals can vary from simple prayer to elaborate ceremonies, but in all cases, rituals honor people's experiences and give them permission to take their experience seriously.

Some Rituals Surrounding Trauma

After collective traumas or individual traumatic deaths, I am astounded to observe how often people create makeshift shrines of flowers, messages, and candles. There are large tributes at the sites of mass killings, and there are small crosses along the sides of highways. This is a secular age, a time when traditional religious rituals are performed less often and are less widely embraced than in the past. And yet, this need to ritualize, to symbolize, to memorialize seems to run deep in the human psyche, whether people are religious or not. It is what my colleague Herbert Anderson calls the "ritual imperative."[14] It emerges spontaneously in the aftermath of a tragedy as a way to honor the dead, as a way of expressing sorrow, even as an effort to bring some meaning to a meaningless event. Most of all, rituals emerge as a way of naming the experience. Although the impulse to ritualize the moment is universal, the forms and formats of trauma rituals are varied, personalized, and informal. This is true whether the rituals are personal or public.

Most of the rituals associated with trauma are quite personalized. They are crafted in the moment for the moment. Examples of rituals include the chaplain praying with a soldier on the battlefield; the minister spontaneously singing to a dying patient; families bringing flowers to the site of a crash; the trauma survivor repeating the twenty-third psalm over and over again; the bereaved family member writing a poetic tribute; and civic leaders gathering around the flag. The circumstances vary widely. Rituals are effective partly because they draw upon traditional words, customs, symbols, and practices. Their form and format may be tailored to the moment, but they are tapping into deep roots in the culture or religious tradition. That is the challenge that ministers face these days, to find the balance between the need to personalize the ritual to the moment and circumstances and the need to employ commonly accepted symbols and practices. People in the midst of trauma need the comfort that comes from the personalization and the safety of established structures and norms.

On the eve of a trauma or in the midst of an ongoing trauma, rituals tend to focus on deliverance, on a miracle, on staying safe, and, if necessary, on preparing for death. In the context of threat, a common ritual is a blessing or anointing ceremony. Ministers perform blessing or anointing rituals, usually assuming a priestly role, and pray *over* another. The Exodus story

---

14. Anderson and Foley, *Mighty Stories, Dangerous Rituals*, 22.

offers another interesting ritual. The children of God were spared trauma when the angel of death "passed over" their marked doorways. The ritual protected them or at least was the mark of a protecting God. It was a ritual created for the unique needs of the moment, as so many trauma-related rituals are. Yet, this ritual offers images and metaphors that ministers might employ today in the context of threat. The metaphor of passing over, or the larger concept of deliverance, speaks to the needs of people caught in trauma.

Some traumas do not include a loss of life per se. Some people escape with their lives. They do not die, even though they might be damaged emotionally and physically. Examples of such situations might include people recovering from an explosion, a violent crime, torture, or sexual assault. There are no prescribed, formal rituals for such situations other than prayers of thanksgiving. The psalms are a rich resource for trauma-based prayers and rituals. In particular, many psalms give thanks to God for deliverance—deliverance from death, from sickness, and from suffering.

Conclusion

In this initial chapter, I have tried to survey the dynamics of trauma, touching on the basic concepts and constructs of trauma and its impact upon us. It is difficult to draw universal conclusions because trauma events vary so widely in kind and degree. People also vary widely in their vulnerability to trauma's impact. Yet, clearly, trauma is more prevalent and pervasive in our times. To be skilled and sensitive caregivers, ministers must understand the basic dynamics of trauma. It is the challenge of our times to respond to trauma with compassion and wisdom, to stand with people in their hour of threat, and to then to shepherd people along into recovery.

Questions for Personal Reflection

1. What trauma(s) have you been through in your life? How does your traumatic experience fit the criteria for trauma given in this chapter? For example, in what way was your experience life-threatening?
2. Find five traumas in the Bible, including individual, collective, and prolonged traumas.

3. Find five different definitions of trauma. Compare them to the definition suggested in this chapter.
4. What is the relationship between trauma and drama? How has the media shaped our experience and appreciation of trauma?
5. In what sense is trauma both an objective reality and a subjective reality? How might this distinction shape trauma's impact?
6. Given the three types of trauma—natural disasters, accidents, and intentional violence—how might a given trauma event be perceived as belonging in one category or another, and why might that perception be important? Why would it be easier for trauma survivors to recover if they perceive a trauma as a natural disaster or an accident rather than an intentional human act?
7. Is bullying a type of trauma?
8. There have been several mass shootings in the United States in recent years. Watch a reputable documentary about one of them and analyze it the event in terms of the dynamics of trauma.
9. If you identify with a particular racial or ethnic group, how has trauma shaped your group's identity?
10. What kinds of prayers would you find helpful in the midst of trauma?

2

Recovery

Trauma is a blow. Trauma is like being hit by a two-by-four across the side of the head. Trauma is like being body slammed, lying there on your back with the breath knocked out of you. Trauma is being stunned. Trauma is being in shock. Recovery, on the other hand, is about recuperating from this shock. It is about taking deep breaths again. It is about recovering from your injuries. It is about stabilizing your life. It is about getting back to normal.

Recovery takes many forms and has many intensities, depending on the severity and type of trauma and the vulnerabilities of the people impacted. Recovery is a process. It may take a few hours or a few years; for a few people, it may take a lifetime. Recovery can also follow idiosyncratic pathways, some of them more indirect than others. This chapter describes the common stages, dynamics, and elements of trauma recovery. Ministers and other Christian caregivers need to understand recovery work so they can better support and encourage people on this important journey.

Safety First

In the immediate aftermath of a trauma, the first task is the restoration of safety, getting people (and ourselves) out of harm's way. If ministers are witnesses to a collective trauma, their first job, like all people of good will, is to assist the authorities and first responders in making sure people are safe. Ministers can mobilize their congregations to help in this task. Congregations often play a significant role in providing emergency shelter, food services, and protection. Normally, religious people are very good at rallying others in times of community crisis to help in recovery.

If the trauma at hand is not a natural disaster or a single event but is an ongoing abusive situation, establishing safety is a bit trickier. If a woman comes seeking pastoral services and she is in a regular, ongoing relationship of physical abuse, a minister's first concern must be her safety and that of her children, if there are any. Ministers may want to consult with social services. Ministers will want to know about the resources for emergency shelters that are available in their communities. In some situations, ministers will need to contact the protective authorities if they suspect that the woman's life is at risk. If the care-seeker resists or refuses professional assistance or the situation is not urgent, ministers may at least be able to help the woman develop an emergency plan, if and when her life is again threatened. Any recovery from trauma cannot begin until she is in a safe place. In fact, attempting to normalize an ongoing abusive relationship is counterproductive. Safety always comes before recovery can begin. Similar protocols would apply to any person, whether an adult or a child, who is living in an ongoing life-threating or abusive situation.

Stabilization and Normalization

In the immediate aftermath of a trauma or release from a traumatic situation, or after any significant traumatic loss event, trauma professionals advise people to stabilize their lives—to return to a regular sleep/wake pattern, meal schedule, and exercise routines. This guidance also means being in an environment that is familiar and normal. There is a sense of safety and trust in being in a familiar setting and following familiar routines. For religious people, this can include various spiritual routines, such as prayer practices. If regular worship attendance is a familiar routine, then congregants should be encouraged to attend weekly services of worship. Other believers may wish to take a break from worship for a time, if worship is too upsetting in some way. Doing the familiar and being in a familiar environment help people establish a sense of normalcy after experiencing something that was very abnormal, out of the ordinary, and maybe even surreal.

Most people discover in the process of trauma recovery or significant bereavement that life gets very simple . . . in a good way. Modern life can be very complicated. The many things that we worry about and the activities that fill up our lives are suddenly not so important. In trauma recovery, people tend to return to the basics of life: eat, sleep, and clean up. They focus on the simple tasks of living. Indeed, sometimes it is all some people can do for awhile. That's okay. They are glad to be alive and enjoying the simple pleasures of living again.

Trauma recovery invites people to again simplify, to focus on what really matters. Material things are not so important any more, especially if the traumatized lost most of their possessions in the trauma. Family is important. Love is important. In fact, life itself is important. Trauma recovery prompts people to simplify life for awhile. Simplifying is like taking a "time out," forgetting all of the pressures, expectations, and tasks of living and just "being" for a while. It is a way of stabilizing and normalizing life and thus feeling safe. It is also an opportunity to experience again a great spiritual truth of the value of the simple life.

Bassel van der Kolk, in *The Body Keeps the Score*, documents the many ways that the body—not just the mind or emotions—is impacted by trauma. He argues that the first step in trauma recovery is not always talking it out but physical grounding. This principle is particularly true for people recovering from severe or prolonged trauma and/or for people whose body was injured or violated in the course of the trauma. In the immediate aftermath of a severe trauma or release from a prolonged trauma, caregivers should encourage people to focus on the nurturing of their bodies. In this regard, people might find yoga, intense exercise or sports, and/or music or dancing helpful. Some people might find it helpful to engage in physical labor. Others might like to nurture their bodies with massages, good food, plenty of sleep, and tender loving care. As I discuss below, people can also reground themselves in their bodies through deep meditation and relaxation exercises. Before people can talk it out, sometimes they need to work it out in their bodies, thereby releasing the "freeze" response or pent-up tension associated with the trauma. Traumatized bodies are wired for action. Body work helps people stabilize and normalize their physiology. It can help them "embody" themselves again, especially if the trauma disconnected them from their bodily experiences.

Anxiety Management

By definition, trauma is a situation or event that causes intense fear, usually because it is a life-threatening event or situation. In the immediate aftermath of trauma or release from a prolonged trauma, fear continues for a time and then is gradually generalized into anxiety.[1] People in a state of acute anxiety feel panic, tension, irritability, and the anticipation that something (else) bad is about to happen. Acute anxiety has somatic manifestations: restlessness, shortness of breath, cold or sweaty hands, heart palpitations, fatigue, dizziness, and perhaps tremors. When people experience these kinds of physiological conditions, they can panic further, thus reinforcing and escalating their anxiety levels. Anxiety has a way of feeding on itself. The mind runs wild; people worry that the threat may happen again or that their body is injured in ways they do not understand. Any medical symptoms, even if they are anxiety-induced, should be taken seriously because they might trigger or intensify preexisting health problems. People will need to consult a medical professional. Some will need medication on a long-term basis to help manage their anxiety. Others will only need medication to get through periods of acute anxiety.

> *Since being robbed and sexually assaulted a few months ago, Heather has been struggling with bouts of anxiety. Her therapist taught her mindfulness meditation. Using a CD as a guide, she has been practicing it twice a day, twenty minutes at a time. She is not very good at it, but she can see how it helps. But just yesterday, in her first support group meeting, she heard the trauma stories of other victims, all of which spiked her anxiety through the roof. She kept taking deep breaths and centering her thoughts until she got home, where she could turn on the CD again and systematically de-escalate. As she says, she is not very good at it, but it helps.*

The most severe acute anxiety usually occurs in the immediate aftermath of a traumatic event, but periods of acute anxiety might also show up throughout the recovery process. Some people, like Heather in the above vignette, may struggle with occasional anxiety attacks, usually triggered by a memory or reminder of the trauma. Others may be retraumatized by a situation similar to the original trauma, thus spiking their anxiety levels momentarily. Still others will experience heightened levels of generalized anxiety that seems to pervade every aspect of their lives. The trauma-related anxieties of some people may be compounded by the environments in which they currently live and work. Others may have a hard time feeling safe because of where and how they grew up; their trauma-related anxiety

---

1. In this chapter, I am distinguishing between fear and anxiety. Fear is more specific, whereas anxiety is more general. Obviously, both feelings are psychophysiological reactions to threat or danger, and they tend to overlap dynamically.

goes to their core, reactivating their earlier primal trust and attachment issues. For some people, the anxiety will run deep. In any event, learning to manage their anxiety is an important first step and a continuous challenge for people recovering from trauma.

Professional trauma therapists note that learning to manage anxiety is almost a prerequisite for successful trauma recovery work. Before people can tell the story of their trauma, which is the heart of recovery work, they need to be able to manage their anxiety. There are several components to learning to manage trauma-related anxiety. First, people may need medications to help reduce their level of anxiety low enough to be manageable. Second, people need to learn to recognize their "triggers," those places, words, sights, memories, people, or even smells that remind them of the trauma and thus raise their anxiety levels. And third, people need to learn various self-soothing or stress-reduction techniques that can be employed both generally and in response to a specific trigger. Mindfulness meditation, as employed by Heather in the above vignette, is one example of an anxiety-reduction technique. By mastering these techniques, traumatized people can begin the process of remembering and sharing their trauma story without being retraumatized. For people recovering from severe trauma or for people whose memories are only partial, this anxiety management work is essential and may appropriately delay for months the process of talking about what happened. In such cases, the process of remembering escalates their anxiety; they must be able to de-escalate themselves and/or manage their fears in ways that prevent them from being overwhelmed again. For other people with relatively mild traumatization or whose memories of the trauma are relatively intact, this anxiety management process will not be as crucial and will not take as long. Still, learning to manage anxiety is a good thing for everyone in recovery work because anxiety is a regular companion throughout the process of recovery and even the grief work that follows.

Spiritual Strategies for Managing Anxiety

The Christian faith has a long tradition of experience and wisdom related to managing anxiety. "Fear not" and "God is our refuge" are regular themes throughout the Bible, and our spiritual ancestors have developed proven ways to help believers experience greater inner peace and courage. I review here some spiritual resources that caregivers and ministers might teach to or cultivate in people who are trying to manage the anxiety associated with trauma. These strategies are not intended to replace professional and medical assistance but may serve as a supplement to such support. They are most effective at preventing panic episodes rather than as interventions once panic attacks have already started. They are, nevertheless, tried and true tools for managing anxiety.

Prayer

Prayer is a traditional way for believers to calm themselves by surrendering their fears and anxiety to God and opening themselves up to receiving God's inner peace. Just verbalizing one's fears in the context of prayer can be calming in and of itself. It is calming, I believe, because a prayerful mind-set is an attitude of surrender; it involves surrendering one's fears and anxieties, which allows one to let go of the need to control or censor one's feelings. In addition to this generalized attitude of surrendering, it is also true that certain types of Christian prayer practices are focused directly on calming the disquieted soul. One of these prayer practices is called centering prayer, which is a form of Christian meditation. In centering prayer, one begins by sitting still, breathing slowly and deeply, allowing one's mind to quiet and one's heart to open up to the presence of God. Sometimes the repetition of a particular word is helpful to recenter oneself when the mind starts to wander. As one goes deeper in prayer, one becomes calmer. The sense of God's presence has a way of calming one's fears, replacing them with a keen sense of the peace that passes all understanding.

Guided Imagery Work

In the context of prayer, many people of faith have used their imagination to create a mental safe place, a place of peace and security. Imagine a safe place, embellish it, cultivate it, and fill it with religious symbols, people, and scenes that create a sense of peace and nurture. Some Christians find it helpful to imagine Jesus present in their safe place, comforting and conversing with them. Sometimes it is helpful to imagine a way of entering one's safe place, such as a passage, a doorway, or a pathway. As one travels to the safe place, the fears and anxieties melt away, replaced by the serenity of this special place. It takes a little practice, but the advantage of an imaginary safe place is that it goes with the believer and is accessible anywhere and anytime.

Scripture Reading

Chronic anxiety is sustained by chronic negative thoughts. Anxious thoughts are generally negative thoughts, judgmental thoughts, exaggerated thoughts, rigid thoughts, or generalizing thoughts ("If it happened once, it will happen again"). Thoughts are important. Changing how people think, from negativity and distortions to more neutral or hopeful thoughts, can calm anxieties.[2] When people pair positive thoughts with existing negative thinking, the positive thoughts can gradually push aside the anxiety by creating new neuropathways in the brain.

The faithful have traditionally dealt with the cognitive aspects of anxiety through Scripture reading. The reading or reciting of Scripture passages can offer comfort, reassurance, and hope. Scripture focuses the reader on cognitions or reassuring thoughts that counter the fears associated with trauma and trauma recovery. Believers may have favorite calming and comforting passages of Scripture. Comforting passages may come in the form of stories, parables, biblical characters, letters, or sermons. The important thing is that they should be passages that emphasize trusting God's goodness in the context of trauma, suffering, and tragedy.

Content and process are both important. When content is blended with process, the impact is more effective. The Lord's Prayer has great content, especially the line "Thy will be done." The process of reciting the Lord's Prayer can also be calming. Christians, for example, can pray the Lord's Prayer in a meditative or contemplative manner, i.e., praying one phrase at a time and, with each phrase, inviting God's peace to dwell within. The well-known and beloved twenty-third psalm can also be recited or prayed in the same fashion. The blending of process and content works well in calming anxieties.

---

2. Pastoral theologians have written extensively about the role of thoughts in anxiety. For example, see Cole Jr., *Be Not Anxious*.

Music

In times of crisis, trauma, or traumatic loss, when anxieties can run high, music is also a good resource for calming the mind. Musical tastes vary according to the individual and the religious tradition, but most believers find certain songs or hymns soothing and calming. Ministers can encourage people to listen to their favorite spiritual songs regularly while recovering from trauma. Ministers can even invite people to sing or hum these songs, letting the soothing melodies calm the soul. Some people may prefer classical music, especially symphonies. Some classical music is wonderfully soothing. Personally, I like lullabies, such as "Tender Shepherd." In times of trauma and loss, drawing on music from childhood has a way of rekindling the experience of basic trust. Indeed, in times of crisis, trauma, and loss, we all come as children to our heavenly parent.

The rhythmic nature of music may account for some of its calming effect on people. What do mothers do to calm infants? They sing and rock them to sleep. Other rhythmic movements or repetitive behaviors can be equally calming. Some people like to say the rosary when they are anxious. Others find chanting helpful. Still others find dancing or swaying to music soothing. The more the lyrics (content) and the melody (process) can work together, the greater the calming effect.

Nature

Some people find nature to be very calming and de-stressing. Walking, hiking, or camping in wilderness areas helps to restore people's sense of trust and order. The beauty and order of creation reminds people of God's goodness. It is restorative. It is also a way of simplifying life. Nature has a way of quieting the soul.

Spiritual practices for managing anxiety, especially contemplative prayer, take some practice if they are to be effective tools for calming or managing one's anxiety. Ministers and other caregivers must be able not only to teach but also to model such practices in their own spiritual lives. Most people cannot learn spiritual practices from a book or a lecture or even from a Bible study, however well taught. They need the patient teaching and personal modeling of a spiritual director. Spiritual practices must be, well, "practiced" to be effective. Although congregants can learn particular practices from their ministers, they must also find the modes and formats that work best for them. Trauma recovery can be a time of deepening one's spiritual walk. One of the key pathways to drawing close to God is through various spiritual practices that help traumatized persons manage their fears and anxiety.

Restoring Trust

By its very definition, trauma is a life-threatening and largely unexpected event. It creates terror to one degree or another and in various durations. Trauma forces people into a helpless state, either momentarily or for a longer period of time, and this returns people to a childlike state and mind-set, to a time when they were dependent and vulnerable. In creating a state of vulnerability, the experience of trauma can reactivate one's earlier primal conflict surrounding trust and mistrust. Trauma has a way of shaking the foundations of the human personality and undermining people's sense of basic trust, which is "the cornerstone of a healthy personality."[3] Some people come through this shake-up with their sense of trust intact, maybe even deepened in some ways. For others, it will be a struggle, maybe even a lifelong struggle, to restore their sense of trust. To one degree or another, everyone experiences a significant trauma as a violation of trust, as a crisis of faith. Recovery for most people must include the restoration of a sense of trust or, at the very least, a wrestling with trust issues.

Trust issues manifest in several dimensions: as trust in God, as trust in self, and/or as trust in others. The type of trauma experienced narrows the focus of a person's crisis of trust. For people recovering from a natural disaster or a medical trauma, their sense of mistrust or betrayal may be focused on God, who they believe should have protected them, or on nature, which is normally predictable, orderly, and nurturing. For people recovering from a traumatic accident, their sense of mistrust may focus on the failure of the government to protect them or of physicians to save them from permanent disability, or it may focus on particular locations or activities ("I will never trust the airlines again"). For people recovering from a trauma caused by another human being, their sense of mistrust can be strong, partly because of what the perpetrator did and partly because he or she may have been a trusted colleague, friend, or member of the family. The sense of betrayal can be strong. People can feel their ability to trust has been shattered.

3. Erikson, *Childhood and Society*, 251.

Recovery

Talking to a Chaplain

Many chaplains serve people on the front lines of trauma, particularly military chaplains, hospital chaplains, police chaplains, fire chaplains, and disaster chaplains. Many people come out of a trauma requesting to "talk to a chaplain." Generally, chaplains have a good reputation as professionals who can be trusted. Chaplains are normally outside of the chain of command or the institutional hierarchy. Therefore, they are persons who are more likely to keep confidences and honor the privacy of individuals. And, of course, they are normally perceived as caring, kind, and supportive. It is very important that the first person traumatized people talk to is trustworthy. This helps restore their ability to trust, which is very important in the aftermath of trauma.

In contrast to a congregational minister, chaplains may also be perceived as more theologically neutral. They usually do not have a theological agenda. They do not have any expectations or carry the pressure of the person's home church or denomination. More and more chaplains are being trained to be interfaith and to be able to respond to any person in need, regardless of their religious affiliation. In many cases, chaplains do not have a previous or continuous relationship with the traumatized person or family. Their conversations are normally short-term. There is something to be said for talking with someone who is totally neutral. Some people find it easier to open up to someone they have not met before and will never see again. Many traumatized persons remember with affection the supportive and kind presence of the chaplain who was there for them when their world fell apart.

Trusting a Therapist

This is the third time Trisha has been identified as suicidal and transported to the local hospital. She has been cutting herself with razor blades, pencils, and scissors. The marks up her arms are easy to notice. In therapy sessions, she avoids talking about her family upbringing, particularly the years of sexual abuse by her grandfather, verbal abuse by her mother's boyfriend, and sense of maternal abandonment. Parts of her childhood she cannot remember; other parts she does not want to remember. She does not know why she cuts herself. "I guess I like feeling the pain . . . at least I am alive." Her

> *therapist has been a godsend—a steady, patient, caring adult who will protect her, even from herself.*

Some traumatized people do not feel comfortable talking to a chaplain or may not have access to chaplaincy services. Their initial contact is with their family, friends, congregational minister, or therapist. Professional psychotherapists are trained to provide a psychologically safe relationship where people can talk about what happened and share all of their related feelings. Therapists create a psychologically safe environment characterized by unconditional positive regard. Therapists who are trained in trauma work can also be helpful guides, providing information, resources, and techniques for managing anxiety and stabilizing one's life. Therapy has many advantages, particularly for people with preexisting psychological vulnerabilities or people passing through severe traumas. But not everyone is comfortable talking to a professional, nor can everyone access therapy due to limitations related to availability and cost.

Establishing a trusting relationship with at least one other person is very important in trauma recovery, as suggested in the above vignette. It is also one of the hardest things for some people to do, precisely because their capacity for trust has been shaken or perhaps because they have a pretrauma dislike of asking for help of any kind. So, people can resist going to see a "shrink." Yet, everyone who is going to go through hell, as trauma recovery work can be, needs their Virgil, someone to companion them on their journey, guide their footsteps, and bear witness to their suffering.[4] Ministers are rarely equipped to be professional Virgils. Rather, their more important role is to serve as a bridge, to connect people to an appropriate and trustworthy mental health professional. If traumatized people trust their minister, they will be more likely take the referral and benefit from the assistance.

People who have been traumatized by violent crime require special sensitivities regarding trust issues. Ministers and spiritual caregivers need to pay special attention to the safety and privacy of the physical location where pastoral services are provided. They must be aware of how their physical presence, gender, age, personality traits, and personal history with the traumatized victim may foster trust or distrust. They must also be sensitive to issues regarding physical touch. In times of trauma, people instinctively want to be hugged, held safe by a loved one, or, in some extreme

---

4. Dante's *Inferno* tells the story of Dante's journey through hell, guided by the ancient Roman poet Virgil.

cases, by any caring person. If the trauma is a natural disaster, hugs can be more freely given and received, but if the trauma is at the hands of someone whom the victim used to trust, it is harder for the victim to seek, much less ask for, a hug. In such cases, hugging without asking permission could be retraumatizing. Establishing trust is very important. In fact, it is central to the recovery process. Compassionate and wise ministers, chaplains, and other spiritual caregivers must be sensitive to the trust issues of traumatized people.

The Power of Community

In the previous chapter I described the various automatic physiological changes in the human body that occur when people perceive extreme and sudden threat. That set of changes has been referred to as the "fight-or-flight syndrome," which is an apt way of describing what these changes are designed to mobilize people to do. Some researchers have suggested that this behavioral description has a male orientation.[5] Females, who react largely the same way as males on a physiological level when under threat, actually "tend and befriend" more than "fight or flight," and this tending and befriending had as much of an evolutionary advantage for females as fighting and fleeing did for males. By and large, women are programmed to respond to threat by connecting with others, drawing on them and giving support, and tending to the needs of children and other adults. In order to tend and befriend, women also verbalize more in times of stress than men typically do. These descriptions, however, are generalizations. The tend-and-befriend response is more typical of females but is not exclusive to women, and the fight-or-flight response is more typical of males but is not exclusive to men. As I see it, these two responses are inherent, evolutionarily formed impulses in all of us to one degree or another. When under threat, people are as likely to band together as to stand and fight . . . or to do both. The point here is that there is a natural and restorative impulse to band together and to seek community in times of trauma or threat that is mostly obviously manifested in women but is also present in all humans. In other words, trauma has a way of reminding us that we need each other.

Stories abound of people in the middle of crisis, war, natural disasters, or any prolonged oppression coming together in genuine, compassionate,

---

5. This concept was first described by UCLA scholar Shelley Taylor and colleagues. See Taylor et al., "Biobehavioral Responses."

and mutually supportive communities. Human beings long for genuine community and are healthiest when living in community. Modern life, especially its mass, impersonal, and urbanized features, tends to undermine community and/or create fragmented communities. Trauma has a way of breaking through all of the social, political, and psychological walls that divide people and force people to work together, in many cases just to survive. Trauma has a way of leveling the playing field. Trauma has a way of bringing humanity back to its roots as a social, tribal species. One of the paradoxical things about trauma is that trauma tends to create community. It tends to create its own antidote.

> *At the National Center for PTSD, sponsored by the US Department of Veterans Affairs, veterans participate in day programs or residential programs that address their chronic PTSD. In the Men's Trauma Recovery Program, one of the unofficial programs is a weekly men's choir that sings mostly old favorites, sentimental and patriotic songs. The choir is the inspiration of a VA chaplain with musical training, and she directs the choir. Each session ends with the singing of "Amazing Grace," during which several of these men, who do not open up or talk much in therapy groups, cry.*

Journalist Sebastian Junger, in his recent book *Tribe: On Homecoming and Belonging*, explores the question, Why do large-scale disasters produce such mentally healthy conditions? Referring to the work of Charles Fritz, he concludes that "modern society has gravely disrupted the social bonds that have always characterized the human experience" and that "disasters thrust people back into a more ancient, organic way of relating. Disasters . . . create a 'community of sufferers' that allows individuals to experience an immensely reassuring connection to others."[6] One of the more common examples of the role of community in the midst of trauma is on the battlefield. Small, cohesive units of soldiers, bonded together with common purpose and genuine mutuality, work together to prevent and mitigate the impact of the traumas of war. Junger suggests that one aspect of the trauma experienced by returning American soldiers is the disruptive loss of that battlefield community when they are discharged back into modern civilian life. The restoration of community in the form of veterans' support groups, such as the one described in the above vignette, is one tool that helps these young men and women recover from the trauma of war. Members of the military are more inclined than most people to want to "tough it out," but

---

6. Junger, *Tribe*, 53.

in the context of battlefield trauma even military personnel appreciate the value of community and cherish its healing power.

Some people are fortunate enough to have family and friends who are supportive and available in times of trauma; others have less support. The mere presence of people alone is not enough, although it helps. More precisely, it is the quality of that support that makes one's community, family, or church community restorative or not. Communities that are available, empathetic, nonjudgmental, authentic, and supportive are laboratories of recovery. Yet traumatized people need more than mere empathy, as wonderful as empathy is. In the early phases of trauma recovery, some traumatized people can be quite unstable and desperate. They might need to lean on others, to borrow their strength, maybe even to be carried emotionally or even literally for a while by family and friends until they can stand on their own two feet again. The most effective kind of community is one that blends support and mutual trust with a strong identity, a common purpose, clear values, and stability over time. Such communities become environments in which traumatized persons can experience trust and safety and begin the recovery process. They are also good places to overcome fear and anxiety. If humans stand together, arm in arm, they can often face their fears.

Trauma Support Groups

The presence and availability of a supportive community of people, whether friends, family, or colleagues, is one of the most important factors in the success of trauma recovery. Small, close-knit groups of people with a common purpose and a commitment to mutual aid and support enable their members to weather and recover from unspeakable horrors. They do so because the web is stronger than its individual strands. Together, the community has the strength to absorb the blow of a trauma, whereas individuals who are alone in the face of trauma can crumble.

Having a traumatized person in a family or in a small church can be taxing. Most ministers and other congregational caregivers want to help, but they may lack the skills, patience, time, and emotional resources to sustain a prolonged relationship with a traumatized person. So it is, then, that the preferred vehicle for providing community for people recovering from trauma is support groups.

A trauma support group is a group of people who have all been traumatized and who meet for a designated period of time for mutual support, assistance, and recovery. Such groups are often comprised of people who have experienced a particular type of trauma, such as rape, a natural disaster, combat, or childhood abuse. Sometimes they are also gender-specific or age-specific. Trauma support groups might be available in the days immediately after a trauma or later as an ongoing recovery group. Because traumatized people can be unstable and/or medically fragile, especially in the early days after a trauma or release from trauma situation, most trauma recovery groups exist under the umbrella of a hospital, mental health clinic, or governmental agency, such as the VA or a military base.

Trauma support groups are effective for a variety of reasons.

- They are safe places, safe physically and safe emotionally. They are confidential and often anonymous. They are nonjudgmental, supportive, and empathetic.
- Participants feel that the other group members "have been there" and therefore understand what they have been through better than non-traumatized persons do. Recognizing the universality of trauma and trauma symptoms helps participants feel normal.
- They are holding environments where people can talk through the varied emotions that accompany recovery. Trauma emotions are often strong emotions. They are also often ambiguous emotions: love and hate, anger and sorrow, relief and sorrow. It is safer to share such strong and ambiguous emotions in a small, structured environment.
- They can easily evolve into or concurrently function as grief support groups and help participants do the necessary grief work that accompanies most traumas.
- They give participants the opportunity to not only receive support but to give it as well. Love heals . . . both when it is received and when it is given. Altruism, when appropriate, aids in the recovery process.
- They share information, provide resources, and serve as vehicles of psychosocial education.

Trauma support groups are not for everyone. Some people still require or do better in a one-to-one relationship with a personal trauma therapist. Some feel embarrassed sharing their personal sufferings in front of a group. Some religious people might prefer a more explicitly Christian context for their recovery work. Others note that support groups are "artificially created" and temporary. Indeed, they are no substitute for the ongoing support of family, friends, and congregation, but the artificially created nature of a support group, if done well, leads to a focus and intensity that makes it an effective tool for trauma recovery. Support groups are effective because they create genuine community, and community is restorative. Ministers and other Christian caregivers can be most helpful by connecting traumatized people to appropriate support groups and encouraging them to join.

Children, Trust, and Family Support

The importance of trusting relationships is even greater when it comes to children who have been traumatized. Children need to feel safe and secure in a family environment in order to recover from trauma. Children also need adults around them who can explain and interpret trauma events for their young minds. Surrounded and supported by their family, children can be quite resilient. Children without families, or children whose families are the cause of their trauma, have a more difficult time recovering and are at risk for a variety of psychological, social, and medical ailments even years later as adults.[7] In the United States, foster care homes are tasked with providing support and stability for traumatized children. Foster parents strive to create a stable, supportive family environment that allows children to regain trust in others and to reconnect to their community. When it comes to trauma, however, we are all children. We all need a community of safe, trustworthy, stable adults in which to recover. Congregations can and should also be places where children can feel safe among trustworthy adults.

Trauma Stories: Remembering What Happened

There is some debate among professionals about how soon the victims/survivors of a trauma should begin talking about what happened. The professionals associated with the Critical Incident Debriefing program argue that it is best to get people talking about what happened immediately after the trauma—within hours after they are safe. They often refer to "the wet

---

7. I noted this in chapter 1. This has been dramatically documented by the Adverse Childhood Experience Study.

cement theory," which suggests that the human memory is like wet cement immediately after a trauma. Debriefing helps people get the story straight and accurate from the onset. Without debriefing, their distorted and fragmented memories of what happened might get set in cement and thereby become more difficult to unravel later in the recovery process. The Critical Incident Debriefing approach is often employed with and seems to be most effective with first responders after a collective trauma and with the survivors of a single-event trauma. Professionals who work with the victims of long-term trauma, such as torture, domestic violence, or human trafficking, argue that these people often cannot always talk about their experience immediately upon release because it is too upsetting, even retraumatizing. It is better for them to focus on stabilizing their lives, reducing somatic distress, and learning to manage anxiety symptoms first. Then, once they are in a safe situation and in the context of a trusted relationship, they can begin the process of talking through what happened. Generally speaking, however, all professionals do agree that, sooner or later, trauma victims/survivors need to remember and tell their story of what happened.

Traumatic Amnesia

> *John is a soldier who was recently evacuated from "down range" after his unit was attacked by rockets and mortars. He is now recovering in a rear guard base in Germany. He was diagnosed with traumatic brain injury, caused by the blasts, and his physical injuries are minor compared to his mental injuries. He struggles with fragments of memories, most loud noises, strong odors, and missing body parts. He paces the floor at night like a lion in a cage. He is tense, irritable, and restless. Just yesterday, the doctors gave him some medication to help him sleep. He hopes it will, but at this point, he actually fears going to sleep.*

One of the problems of people involved in trauma is that they may have been so overwhelmed by the trauma, like John in the above vignette, that they have forgotten much of the event or situation or have only distorted, fragmented memories of the event. They may have partial amnesia, sometimes even full amnesia, which is called "traumatic amnesia." The technical word for the dynamics of traumatic amnesia is dissociation. As described in the previous chapter, dissociation is something the mind does to protect itself when it is overwhelmed. In the midst of trauma, the mind "dissociates" itself from the present moment; one's consciousness "goes somewhere else." One becomes numb, goes into a trance, functions on autopilot, or, in extreme forms, leaves one's body for a time. All of this results in fragmented, distorted, or a complete absence of memories of the trauma event. Dissociation can be strong, moderate, or mild. Dissociation should be understood as being on a continuum that ranges from complete amnesia (strong) to fragmented memories (moderate) to distorted memories (mild).[8]

Information-Processing Model

The impact of trauma upon individuals has been traditionally understood through the lens of psychiatry. In recent years, drawing on the emerging research in neuroscience, another model for understanding the impact of trauma has emerged that can be characterized as an information-processing model. In everyday life, people constantly receive information through their senses—all kinds of data, thoughts, feelings, sensations, perceptions, images, and conversations. These are placed temporarily in the part of the brain called the short-term memory. There the data is sorted out, organized, and coded. The process of adding words and structure to it emotionally decharges the information. Short-term memory also compares this new information to existing memories, meanings, and schemas. The information deemed important is then filed in long-term memory, and the irrelevant information is simply forgotten. In the long-term memory, information is organized and classified for easy retrieval. This is, in brief, the memory formation process.

In trauma situations, people are bombarded with a great deal of emotionally charged data, thoughts, feelings, sensations, perceptions, images, and internal somatic reactions. The brain can absorb a lot of information, especially when it is energized and focused on a threat. Yet, for some people in some situations, this flood of intense stimulation is too much. It is traumatic. The surge of information overloads their mental circuits, in particular the capacity of their short-term memory to process information. To use a computer metaphor, it is like trying to force 500 megabytes of data

---

8. In some rare cases, the walled-off memories characteristic of dissociation become semipermanent structures of the personality, resulting in what the *DSM-5* calls dissociative identity disorder or what used to be called multiple personalities. The prevalence of dissociative identity disorder in the general population is 1.5 percent. See American Psychiatric Association, *DSM-5*, 292.

through a bandwidth that is too small to handle it. It is literally too much information ("TMI"). Or to change the metaphor, it is similar to what some would describe as "drinking water from a fire hose." The mind can only process so much. The excess data spills over or outside of the normal neurological channels, going directly into the unconscious as fragmented, disconnected, emotionally charged information. Traumatic memories are thus different from regular memories. They are more fragmented, less verbal, more emotionally charged, and more like a series of disconnected images, impressions, sights, and sounds. The material is emotionally distressing and often does not make sense, and it is certainly not integrated into the larger memory systems of the individual.

Once the crisis has passed, the process of reintegrating this fragmented, disconnected, and emotionally charged information into the conscious mind and then gradually processing it through the normal mechanisms of memory formation can begin. Note the word *gradually*. This painful information needs to be processed at a rate that the mind can handle. Too much information flooding the mind will again overwhelm the capacity of the short-term memory mechanism. Telling one's story, or "storying," thus has an important role in this process. The storying process is by definition a gradual process, a process that transposes the fragmented, charged memories into words and integrates them into a larger narrative or framework of meaning so they can be stored in long-term memory. Storying is the outward manifestation of the inner processes of short-term memory.

How Shall We Remember?

Recovery from trauma requires that people come to terms with what happened. If traumatized people have fragmented memories or partial amnesia, as John does in the above vignette, it can be very frightening. They can easily think that they are losing their mind. Ministers, chaplains, and therapists need to reassure people that these "crazy" reactions are actually normal reactions to an abnormal and frightening event. They need to provide traumatized people with a safe, stable, and trustworthy environment where they can begin, however gradually, to reconstruct their memories and form what is commonly called their "trauma story."

In the process of forming their trauma story, traumatized people need to have a fierce commitment to and passion for the truth, however painful it may be. In so doing, some traumatized people may have to face unpleasant aspects of the situation or themselves. So, truth-seeking requires courage. It is hard because in the face of pain the human mind has a tendency to distort memories, to twist the truth to suit its preexisting understandings of reality, oneself, and others. Recovering people have to be willing to challenge their own biases and perceptions. They should be encouraged to talk to other participants in the trauma, to gather facts not currently known, to gain different perspectives—in short, to be a good investigator.

On a collective level, it is interesting to note that the media perform this same function, trying to get the trauma story straight by investigating and writing down information so that communities can form collective memories. Much of the media's work in times of collective traumas is focused on getting to the truth of what happened and assigning blame and understanding "why" a trauma occurred. If the trauma is caused by a human being, for example, then the media want to know his or her life story, who or what failed this person, who could or should have stopped him or her, and so on. If the trauma is a natural disaster, then the focus is on who did not adequately warn the victims, who did not respond fast enough, who should or could have done something to prevent the disaster, and so on. Getting to the story straight, getting to the truth, helps the community form its collective memory of the trauma and eventually its history.

This same impulse is a component of individual trauma storying, too. People want to get the story right, to know the full truth, partly to know if they were at fault in some way or who else might be at fault. Some people feel quite driven to get the story straight, partly out of their own need to assign responsibility or to be relieved of responsibility. Yet when the full story does come out, the truth is seldom simple. Few traumas are 100 percent the fault of a particular individual. Rather, many people share the responsibility, and a good portion of the responsibility must be assigned to chance. Trying to nail down responsibility can be a futile task. Ministers, particularly those with moralistic leanings, must be careful not to unintentionally fuel this futile task. Sometimes recovery work needs to be understood as learning to live with the ambiguities, learning to be okay with seeing "in a mirror dimly" until such time as we "know fully, even as I [we] have been fully known" (1 Cor 13:12 NRSV).

Journaling

To help get their trauma story straight, many people find regular journaling to be a helpful discipline during their recovery. Journaling includes not just writing down the information as it is remembered or discovered but also writing down one's responses, questions, dreams, and feelings as they occur in connection with the emerging story. Journaling helps traumatized people process information and integrate sometimes distorted and fragmented pieces of information or memories into a linear sequence. Journaling helps traumatized people integrate and process material as it surfaces, thus allowing and facilitating the memory formation process. And writing down emotionally charged memories helps "externalize" them. Generally speaking, the more regular the journaling process, the better. I usually recommend daily journaling for people in the throes of recovery work, and I challenge them to treat it like a spiritual practice.

Bearing Witness to Another's Suffering

In time, the story needs to be told to another human being. After remembering and writing it down, it is important that the story be spoken out loud, that the victims of trauma give voice to their thoughts. There is value in public witness. That public arena could be a trauma support group or it could even take a more indirect approach, such as when artists publish or perform their story. The story is thus is made public. For most people, however, the witnessing is done one to one. The witness can be a judge, a therapist, a reporter, or a clergyperson. Telling one's trauma story to another person may not be very difficult for some people, but for others, whose traumatization is more severe and/or whose trauma is couched in shame, telling their story in public becomes a significant step in their recovery.

It is surprising how important it is to some people to tell their trauma story to a member of the clergy. Even people who have not attended a worship service in years may feel compelled to speak to a clergyperson in the aftermath of a trauma. It seems especially powerful when there is injustice involved or when the suffering seems unbearable. Why is this? I suppose people feel that they are telling their story to God. Like Job, they want to make sure God knows how badly they have suffered or been wronged. In such situations, clergy do more than listen, although listening is foundational and essential. Clergy are also "bearing witness," a sacred task that has deep theological roots in the Christian Scriptures (see Rom 8:16). The verb "to bear witness" is associated with the justice system. Ministers testify truthfully before the Throne of Grace on behalf of another who has suffered so much. This extra dimension, the sense that a minister is bearing witness, receiving, remembering, and testifying to the truth of the trauma story, validates the story in the mind of the storyteller. Having a minister validate the trauma story helps the storyteller validate it, too, and then accept it and even embrace it as their story.

The process of reconstructing the story of what happened and telling the story to at least one other person has another benefit besides story reconstruction. Storying is also a way of managing trauma-related fears and anxieties. Verbalizing their fear helps people face those fears. Labeling it, objectifying it, and externalizing it helps people manage it. It might be said that trauma work is not just about storying but also about befriending the story. "Befriending" does not mean that people like or approve of what happened . . . only that they accept it. People can now talk about the story calmly, objectively, and without intense fear or anxiety, although maybe still with emotion. They are at peace with it. They can remember it well.

Trauma Stories: Discovering What Happened to a Loved One

Trauma triggers anxiety. Even when people are not personally threatened, trauma creates anxiety. For the family shocked by the news of the traumatic death of a loved one, anxiety pervades the initial stages of recovery and grief. One of the typical ways that anxiety emerges is through focusing on how the loved one died.

One of the first questions families ask when notified of the violent death of a loved one is, "What happened?" The second most common question is, "Did my loved one suffer?" In the immediate aftermath of a violent death, the details may not be fully available. In the absence of those details, people imagine the worst. They visualize their loved one's dying. They may have dreams or nightmares on the same theme. The violence and suffering associated with the dying can be difficult for loved ones to accept.

In the days and weeks following the violent death of a loved one, more information usually becomes available. With this additional information, the focus shifts to constructing a story of how the loved one died. If a woman was murdered, her family wants to know the details of her dying.

They want to find out the cause of death, the mechanics of death, the whys and hows of it all. It may be helpful for them to talk to other players in the trauma event, such as police officers and the woman's friends and neighbors. They want to understand the motives of the assailant.

Psychiatrist Edward K. Rynearson argues in his book *Retelling Violent Death*[9] that traumatic grief is different from "ordinary" or anticipated grief in precisely this way. The early stages of recovery are focused on reconstructing the story of how a loved one died. The traumatized family may mentally reenact their loved one's dying again and again. They may become consumed with trying to get the story right, making an incoherent story coherent. Toward this end, family members may gather information, interview first responders and other people who interacted with the deceased, dig through the deceased person's belongings, or visit the site of the tragedy, all in an effort to reconstruct the story of how their loved one died.

Search for Answers

As the details of a loved one's death are uncovered, family and friends may learn that there were large elements of chance or fate attached to their dying. In other words, the deceased was in the wrong place at the wrong time. If there is an element of chance or fate in the traumatic death, the search for answers may shift to bigger questions, such as, "Why now?" "Why my loved one?" "Why did he or she have to die?" Violent death, gruesome suffering, unexpected cruelty, and random bad luck all have a way of challenging people's assumptions about the goodness of humanity, the fairness of life, and/or the love of God. Traumatic losses, more than ordinary losses or natural deaths, tend to sharpen these spiritual questions and issues. Struggling with these questions is not limited to religious people. Almost everyone wonders about these larger questions in the context of traumatic death.

Sometimes families do not like the answers that they find. The truth might be hurtful or embarrassing. Perhaps they discover that there was something more they could have or should have done. Perhaps the way their loved one died or lived is more shameful or embarrassing than previously known. For some people, it is not always helpful to know every detail of their loved one's dying. Families often need the wise counsel of caregivers to recognize the limits and appropriate boundaries of their search for answers.

9. Rynearson, *Retelling Violent Death*, 25.

Recovery

Trauma, Anxiety, and Closure

The Nash family was devastated by the news that their son had been murdered. Almost immediately, they knew that they had to see it for themselves, the site where their son had died in Spain while studying aboard at an art institute. He was murdered, according to the US Embassy, on a popular walking trail outside of town, where he was staked to a tree. They wondered if his murder was some kind of hate crime since their son was openly gay. When they arrived in Spain, they met many of their son's peers at the art institute and interviewed local police. Then they made a pilgrimage along the trail to the tree where the police had found him, and they placed flowers by the tree, pausing to pray and take in the experience. The next day, they escorted their son's body home for his funeral service.

The traumatic death of a loved one is characterized by a sense of unfinishedness. It is so sudden, so unexpected. There is no time to say goodbye. There is no warning, no opportunity for anticipatory grief. Feeling unfinished, bereaved families, like the Nash family in the above vignette, seek a sense of closure. Getting the full story about how a loved one died does provide some closure. Being able to secure the deceased person's body and have it properly buried also helps. Establishing a memorial may help, too. Ultimately, plaques, statues, war memorials, a charitable foundation, or even planting a tree may also provide a sense of closure. Closure is hard to come by when the death is sudden and violent. Some bereaved families may need professional help to complete their unfinished emotional business. Yet, closure begins with establishing and telling the story of the loved one's dying, which in turn, as Rynearson suggests, paves the way for a shift to a focus not on how the loved one died but on how he or she lived—a shift from recovery to bereavement. Until then, anxiety tends to block grief.

Rituals in Recovery

In the immediate aftermath of trauma or news of a traumatic loss, rituals can be very comforting. Rituals aid trauma victims' recovery by providing an emotional "safe place" and by using familiar images, music, visuals, and words that are reassuring and calming. In the early stages of trauma recovery, people need stability, structure, and safety more than emotional expressivity.

Personal rituals, such as daily prayers, readings, and self-care activities, also provide structure, familiarity, and stability. Public rituals provide the additional benefit of a supportive community. Community rituals should provide trauma victims with opportunities to share their experience in a trusting, nonjudgmental environment and in that sharing to develop an honest trauma story. Accepting what happened and being honest about it is essential in the early stages of recovery.

In the early stages of trauma recovery, rituals are helpful when they acknowledge the spoken and unspoken doubts and confusion about why the tragedy happened. Sometimes the traditional theological answers are comforting; many times it is better just to acknowledge the confusion before God and trust that answers will become clearer in time. Unfortunately, ministers can get caught up in the anxiety too and turn prayers into sermons.

Many Christian denominations have formal rituals or worship services for healing. Generally, such rituals can be a helpful resource or tool for facilitating recovery work, but it depends on how they are used. In the context of the aftermath of trauma, such rites can be helpful if

- the focus is not just on physical healing but also on inner peace;
- the ritual assumes that recovery is a process, not a one-time, dramatic event;
- the ritual is used to sustain and encourage people in their recovery work;
- the ritual reinforces the idea that healing is not something done to them by God but something God and people do together as partners; and
- the ritual does not reinforce an absolutist view of God's will.

Many faithful people look with a jaundiced eye at faith healings. The media have given faith healings a bad rap! Yet people in the midst of trauma pray for deliverance without embarrassment. People on the edge of death pray for a miracle. People haunted by fear pray for relief. Ultimately, there is a note of mystery in recovery and healing. The very act of participating in a ritual can itself be a first step in the restoration of faith and inner peace.

Recovery

Incomplete Recovery

Trauma is a life-threating event or series of events. As such, it triggers fear and potentially massive amounts of anxiety. Recovery is about stabilizing one's life, managing anxiety, rebuilding trust, and recovering memories. These are the four primary tasks in recovery work, and they are all interrelated. Ideally, every traumatized person would complete these tasks. Unfortunately, some people do not recover from trauma, or they recover only partially. Many other people do just enough trauma work to feel well enough to return to their "normal" lives. Generally, ministers need to support people's recovery work and urge them to complete it, not rush through it or shortchange it.

Signs of an incomplete trauma recovery include the inability to trust, continuing problems with anxiety that manifest as irrational fears, overcontrolling behaviors, obsessive worrying, overreacting to seemingly ordinary events, and overreliance on alcohol and drugs. Incomplete trauma recovery also makes bereavement difficult, resulting in complicated or prolonged grief. Ministers and lay caregivers can play a helpful role by suggesting to people that these "signs" need to be taken seriously and prompting them to reenter or double down on their recovery work.

Humans are remarkably good at denial. Denial is one of the chief ways that people manage anxiety. It is one of the chief dynamics leading people to avoid, shorten, or drop out of their recovery process. In some ways, denial is necessary. We could not function if we were not able to compartmentalize our anxiety. But denial does not always serve us well. In the case of single-event traumas, including most natural disasters, we are remarkably adept at denial. As soon as an earthquake passes, for example, we "forget" to follow through on recommended precautions to be better prepared for the next one. As soon as the fire is over, and especially if our home was spared, we fail to make the changes required to mitigate a future fire. As soon as the media attention dies down after a mass shooting, the political will to tighten gun control regulation falters. People go on with their lives. In a sense, monuments, museums, and cultural stories are attempts to counter denial's negative thrust by reminding people and future generations of collective traumas, of the tragedies and the lessons learned. Monuments, museums, and stories encourage people to remember so something similar will not happen again. But unfortunately, unless the trauma's lessons are institutionalized, memories tend to fade with each passing generation. Once the threat has dissipated, people tend to compartmentalize their anxiety and go on with their lives.

Denial begins its work fairly soon, even while people are in recovery. Trauma victims can deny the full impact or implications of the trauma, partially because they cannot cope with the anxiety and partially in a determined attempt to "forget it" and move on: "It happened.... I cannot change it," "Just tough it out," "Let's forget it."

Denial is one of the chief psychological blocks to full recovery. Denial leads people to shorten, delay, or only partially complete their recovery work. Instead of learning to manage anxiety, for example, people compartmentalize their anxiety, move on with their lives, telling themselves that it won't happen again, that it wasn't that bad, or that they are as good as new.

One of the other things that leads people to not complete their trauma recovery work is the recovery model itself. "Recovery" implies a return to normalcy. This orientation is especially evident in community traumas. Recovery consists of repairing bridges, rebuilding homes, fixing the power lines ... getting the community functioning and back to normal. Traumatized individuals tend to think the same way: they feel they need to get back to work, heal their wounds, and file insurance claims, and then life will be like it was before. Life will be normal again. As I have already said, many people do just enough of the recovery work to feel normal again, and then they move on with their lives, setting aside the remaining pain, memories, and losses.

Alas, for many traumatized people, recovery is not that simple. In fact, there is no "normal" for them to go back to. Their lives have been permanently altered. In fact, I would argue that this is the case in every trauma, although most people just do not realize it. They do not understand that their lives have been permanently changed. One of the reasons why people are unable to embrace their new (post-trauma) lives is that they have failed to deal with the losses associated with the trauma they experienced. It is to this subject that I turn next.

Questions for Personal Reflection

1. How have you recovered from the traumas or traumatic losses in your life? What helped, and what did not help?

2. Sometimes you have to remember before you can forget. Do you journal on a regular basis? Do you think that journaling might be a way of helping people, perhaps people who are naturally not outgoing, to get their trauma story formed and on paper? What guidelines can you suggest for the best use of journaling?

3. Give some examples of people who have turned their trauma story into a novel, song, or movie script. How is doing so healing not only for the author but also for those who share in their story vicariously as viewers or readers?

4. What spiritual practices would help a person recovering from a trauma restore their sense of trust in God?

5. When and where have you experienced genuine community and/or dysfunctional community? Describe the difference. What helps genuine community form and be sustained?

6. Make a playlist of spiritual music that you find most calming and soothing. Make another list of Scripture passages you find most calming and soothing. Remember that what you find calming may not be what other people find calming, but your list is a good place to start.

7. In your town or city, where do people go who need to be safe? Where do you go to feel safe?

8. How is your congregation prepared to deal with a collective trauma?

9. "If I choose it, it is not a trauma." Reflect on this phrase.

10. What rhythmic activities or experiences do you find calming? Do you play a musical instrument? If not, would you consider learning to do so?

3

Losses

As people remember and share their trauma stories, either stories about what they went through or how their loved one died, they become more aware of what they have lost. People cry as they remember. They cry as they talk. This is precisely why remembering and telling their story is so good for people. Remembering leads naturally into grieving. Recovery evolves into healing.

In this chapter, I touch on the many kinds of losses that are possibly associated with or triggered by a traumatic event. The more significant and obvious losses associated with trauma are termed "traumatic losses," which are different from "ordinary" or "normal" losses (if any significant loss can really be considered ordinary). To phrase it differently, a traumatic loss is a loss embedded in a trauma. Indeed, there are many losses, significant and less significant, embedded in trauma. And what significant loss is not traumatic in some degree? "Traumatic" simply refers to *how* the loss occurs. Any loss that is unexpected, horrific, violent, and/or overwhelming could be experienced as traumatic. But generally the distinguishing feature of traumatic loss is violence or destruction.

Apart from traumatic or violent losses, I argue in this chapter that the losses associated with trauma come in many forms, intensities, and complexities. Some losses are obvious and traumatic—a loved one died, an explosion amputated a person's legs, or an earthquake destroyed a town. Other losses are subtler, hidden, and only come to mind in the course of recovery. All of the losses associated with a trauma event diminish the well-being of those involved. Helping people identify their losses facilitates their movement from trauma recovery to grief work. Too many people fixate on the trauma event, come to define themselves by that horrible event, and never move on to a fuller healing made possible by grief work. A full realization of what they have lost breaks open their hearts and allows God, family, and caregivers to provide a healing touch.

Facing One's Own Death

Death, especially our own death, is the primal fear that haunts all of us at some level. Among the range of losses, death is unique in its finality and inevitability, and therein lies its power and its terror. This unconscious "terror of death," as Ernest Becker termed it, fuels human civilization, culture, and personal character. Our anxiety over death and personal annihilation is so overwhelming that we largely deny its reality. People maintain this denial, argues Becker, through desperate efforts to secure immortality in whatever ways and forms it takes, from art to religion to wealth, from conquest to bearing children and even to heroic acts. Becker continues, "The real world is simply too terrible to admit. It tells man [sic] that he is a small trembling animal who will someday decay and die. Culture changes all of this, makes man seem important, vital to the universe, immortal in some ways."[1] Unfortunately, the denial of death actually robs people of life. To be fully human, to be fully alive, is to accept and transcend this terror with courage. This is the opportunity that trauma presents.

Trauma is by definition an event or events of extreme threat—a knife to the throat, a bomb blast, an airplane crash, a bullet whizzing past one's head. Trauma shatters denial. Trauma blows up personal defenses. Trauma forces people to face their own immortality in the flash of a moment or in the endless torture of days or weeks or years. Trauma makes people face the truth that they so carefully deny most of their lives—that they will die and that "this may be it." Some may have time to think about it, to anticipate it, even to prepare for it. Some may see their life flash in front of their eyes in mere seconds.

Some people escape with their lives, avoiding the ultimate loss embedded in trauma. They might have been robbed or raped but lived to tell the tale. They might have been tortured or abused for years but eventually walked out of that prison. They might have walked away from a serious auto crash, unscathed. They might have been wheeled into the emergency room but walked out under their own power. In such cases and others,

---

1. See Becker, *Denial of Death*, 133.

traumatized people sigh with relief or thank their lucky stars. In these situations, the experience of loss may not be obvious. Yet, people do not walk away from a severe trauma totally unscathed and return to their normal life as if nothing happened. There are losses, such as the loss of one's pre-trauma life, loss of innocence, loss of a sense of security, safety, or control, perhaps even a loss or reduction of health. Writing from the context of prolonged trauma, psychiatrist Judith Herman notes, "Even those who are lucky enough to escape physically unscathed still lose the internal psychological structures of a self securely attached to others."[2] They feel violated. Perhaps they feel they have lost a sense of self or safety. And if people are physically damaged from trauma, even if they are later healed, there is a way in which they will never be the same again. They have lost the sense of their bodily integrity or wholeness. Loss is ever present and integral to the nature of trauma.

Because humanity's anxiety about death is so deep, so pervasive, and normally so well defended against, when trauma triggers its release, the resulting anxiety is equally intense and pervasive. It is overwhelming, sometimes out of proportion to the danger, sometimes immobilizing in its intensity. It is easy to rush back into denial. Yet trauma does present each person with the opportunity to come to terms with reality and to embrace life if they are willing to do the work of recovery and grief. On the other hand, for most traumatized people, trauma is too much reality too fast. So as soon as the threat subsides, they return to the mechanisms of denial and avoidance.

The Death of a Loved One

Trauma is about a threat to life. Loss is about the actual loss of life. Apart from the threat to one's life, one of the dynamics that makes trauma traumatic is the death of a loved one, a friend, a colleague, or any person one cares about. These are the most obvious and intense losses associated with trauma.

Even when it is not due to a traumatic death, people generally experience the death of a loved one as the most significant and upsetting type of loss. The death of loved ones is stressful precisely because they are *loved*. The degree of love generally determines the degree of upset, disruption, and sorrow. Most people, therefore, experience the death of a spouse or the

---

2. Herman, *Trauma and Recovery*, 188.

death of a child as the most difficult loss, precisely because the bonds of love are normally so strong and complex. However, generalizations cannot be made. Some people may be more emotionally bonded to other kinds of human relationships or even to nonhuman entities. Indeed, the "experience of loss" has more to do with the emotional bond or meaning that is assigned to what is now lost.

In the case of trauma, however, the death of a loved one is compounded by the violent and sudden nature of the person's passing. Often people did not expect the loss, even though they might have feared or even suspected it could happen. The violent and sometimes gruesome nature of a death is especially troubling. People's hearts ache knowing that their loved one might have suffered needlessly, experienced terror in the seconds before their demise, or pleaded for mercy or relief with no one there to ease their passage. When a loved one dies in a trauma event, the sense of loss is immediate and overwhelming. Bereaved, traumatized people usually burst open with an intense grief and anxiety reaction.

Secondary Losses

> *It was exactly 6:33 PM on a humid spring evening. The Millers remember it very well because it was the day their lives changed forever. Spring is tornado season on the plains. It was not big as tornadoes go, but the tornado that evening took out their farmhouse and most of their livestock and ripped up the lower fields. The sounds of crashing timbers and shattering glass still ring in their ears and occasionally in their dreams. What they observed when they emerged from the storm cellar was devastating. The Millers spent days picking through their belongings; they were exhausted, hungry, and numb. So much was lost, not just the house and animals but their history, their identity. They celebrated the few, precious photographs or mementoes that they were able to salvage. When they could not afford to rebuild, they also lost their former way of life. Today, the Millers live in an apartment in Phoenix, Arizona.*

A *primary loss* is a significant death or injury or destruction of someone or something triggered by a trauma event. Primary losses are usually tangible losses, losses of something concrete, such as people and property. A *secondary loss* is a loss that comes later as the consequences of the primary loss are played out. In the above vignette, the primary loss is the destruction of the Millers' home by a tornado. This traumatic loss is difficult enough, but it also triggers a cascade of subsequent losses and changes.

Another example might be the death of one's spouse in the prime of life. This loss is difficult enough, but it too may trigger several secondary losses, such as a change of residence because the family home can no longer be sustained, a loss of income without the second breadwinner, the loss of a sex partner, the loss of a co-parent, the loss of or change in the family structure or dynamics, and often the loss of friends because friends who were largely "couple friends" fade away.

A third example might be the plight of refugees, who often leave their homeland after years of being oppressed, even tortured. That is trauma! Then, in leaving their homeland, they experience a significant, multidimensional loss—the loss of home, job, career, and friends. But as the years unfold in their new home, they may experience various secondary losses—the loss of language, the loss of culture, the loss of identity. Refugees, like many people, may underestimate the impact of these secondary losses. Compared to the primary loss or the primary trauma, these losses seem minor, "the least of my problems." People may be glad just to be alive. It is easy to ignore the feelings or stress associated with these changes. These secondary losses, however, can have a cumulative effect, causing more stress and thus a greater impact upon people's health than might be expected if each loss were considered on its own. Furthermore, some people find that their most difficult and stressful challenges are not the primary crisis at all but the many varied losses and necessary adjustments that follow.

Some secondary losses are immediate, but most materialize some time later or their implications become clearer months or even years after the primary loss. Parents who lose a child in a tragic death may experience pangs of grief periodically over the years and/or become aware years later of the impact of that earlier tragedy. Often anniversaries, rituals, and birthdays are the marker events that trigger a flash of sorrow in which parents realize how much they have lost, the son or daughter they no longer have. The dynamic of triggers that reactivate grief is not too dissimilar from the dynamic of triggers that create spikes in anxiety for people recovering from trauma. Many parents report that they never get over the death of a child, especially a traumatic death. It is a loss that lingers through the years.

Continuing the theme of looking at the long-term consequences of trauma and traumatic losses, I remind you of the Adverse Childhood Experiences Study, which I described in the previous chapter. This study confirmed the striking observation that "developmental traumas," which are experienced in the formative years of life, are filled with losses and can have consequences well into the adult years. Children traumatized during their formative years are more likely to experience health challenges, psychological problems, and social adjustment issues well into their adult years. What is true of children is also true, although perhaps to a lesser degree, of adult victims of trauma. Adults who experience severe trauma events are also more susceptible to future psychological difficulties, including problems with addictive behaviors, especially if the embedded losses are not acknowledge or grieved.

The key point here is that losses come in clusters or in strings, especially after a primary traumatic loss. People do not experience any significant loss as an isolated event. The impact of a primary loss moves outward, like ripples in a pond, impacting and triggering other changes and losses. The expanding waves can come in rapid succession, they can cover multiple domains of life, and, as just noted, the waves can continue on in unanticipated ways down through the years. This is why trauma or traumatic loss events can be so significant, especially in the long run. It is not just the primary loss, as difficult as it might be, that makes the effects of trauma powerful; it is also everything else that follows.

Collateral Damage: Relationship Losses

> Luis's six-year-old nephew was killed in a drive-by shooting. It appeared to be an accident of sorts. Bullets meant for someone else went right through the open front door, catching the young boy at play. The family's anguish was intense, visible, and extended. Nothing quite like this had ever happened to them, at least not in America. The funeral proceedings involved the entire extended family. Two of Luis's cousins seemed to know who was responsible, but they were not talking. Several months later, one of the cousins was involved in a fight in the parking lot of the local market, which Luis thinks might have had something to do with the earlier drive-by shooting. About eighteen months later, Luis's sister and brother-in-law broke up. His sister said, "He wouldn't talk about it," and his brother-in-law said, "She was never the same after the shooting."

Many marriages, families, and friendships do not survive the stress of trauma or a traumatic death. The high stress level can magnify existing cracks in intimate relationships, sometimes creating permanent and irreparable ruptures. Marital dissolution is one of the more common types of secondary losses associated with trauma. For example, research reveals that adults with PTSD have a higher rate of marital separation and divorce.[3] Trauma is also highly correlated with related issues such as domestic violence and drug abuse, which are themselves associated with higher rates of marital unhappiness and dissolution. Family therapists report that one of the prevailing issues in intimate relationships, as illustrated in the above vignette, is that partners fail to understand and appreciate the fact that they grieve or manage anxiety differently. It is challenging for partners to maintain an empathetic bond when they cannot see beyond their different coping styles to their mutual deep pain.

It is also true that the experience of divorce itself might be traumatic in its own right, as when a betrayal is discovered or an unexpected request for a divorce is announced. The traumatic nature of some divorces, compounded by anger, resentment, and blame, makes the death of a marriage difficult to grieve. Spouses resist acknowledging their losses as long as they are locked in battle and feel attacked and threatened. Any chance of forming a new, constructive relationship with their ex-spouse for the sake of the children requires that they get past their anxiety and fear so that they can work through the loss and grief associated with the breakup.

Hidden Losses

The word cancer *came as a shock. Mary was just thirty-eight years old and in the prime of life, but, like her mother and grandmother, she had an early diagnosis of breast cancer. Everything happened so fast. It seemed as if, in just a matter of weeks, she went from being a healthy, happy woman to a disfigured woman who was choosing the size of her breast implants. She lost her figure and her health, but there was something else, something more subtle. She also lost her sense of identity and continuity as a person and gained the fear that her husband might not find her attractive any longer, as well as the irrational fear that she was no longer a good enough mother and that this was the beginning of the end of her life.*

---

3. See Jennifer L. Price and Susan P. Stevens, "Partners of Veterans with PTSD," National Center for PTSD, https://www.ptsd.va.gov/professional/treatment/family.

Some of the losses associated with trauma or any significant death are hidden. They are intangible losses, psychological losses, or changes in the human psyche or mind, changes in how people think and define themselves. The above vignette illustrates two common examples: the loss of or change in identity and the loss of the sense of self-worth. In Western culture, most people tend to define themselves largely by their job or their role in the family matrix. Who am I? I am a plumber or a dentist or a grandparent or a wife. We often derive our sense of identity and worth from our work and/or our role in the family. A traumatic loss of health, such as that associated with cancer or any other traumatic loss, might require one to change careers or jobs. It might also require that one function differently in the family matrix. Upon the death of our parents, we often need to recognize that we are no longer a child but the matriarch or patriarch of the family. For some people, these subtle changes in identity or self-definition are experienced as losses.

In popular culture, people use phrases like loss of face, loss of faith, loss of innocence, loss of dreams, loss of youth, loss of history, and even loss of hope. What do people mean by such phrases? Adult survivors of childhood abuse often feel a pervasive sense of loss—that they lost their innocence or their childhood years ago. Some people are so injured or crippled by a trauma event that they lose hope, the hope that they will ever recover, ever be normal again. They might also feel that they have lost their dreams for the future. When a family loses all of their possessions to a fire, they might experience a loss of their history or family identity. They might also feel a loss of independence and security, which are admittedly vague but powerful concepts.

Elections and athletic contests can also involve loss experiences, sometimes even traumatic experiences if the result is unexpected and unwelcomed. The key players or candidates invest time, money, and energy preparing themselves for the competition. And their followers, fans, or supporters, thousands if not millions of them, similarly invest time, money, and energy working for and supporting their chosen team or candidate. And if their favorite candidate or team loses, then there are tears, anger, and despair—all of the essential signs of a significant loss. What is lost here, really? Is it not a shattering of expectations? It is amazing that entities as intangible as expectations, dreams, and even hope can be such powerful losses.

Gruesome Deaths

By definition, trauma includes an element of horror. Trauma is an event that is "out of the ordinary" due to its gruesome or repulsive character. Thus, first responders might be traumatized by picking through body parts or digging up mass graves. A prisoner of war might listen nightly to the screams and cries of those being tortured. A teen caught in human trafficking might have to observe or participate in sexual or violent behaviors that are repulsive. The next of kin might imagine the gruesome nature of their loved one's dying, and in so doing their loss is compounded. "He died in a trash heap, smelling garage," cried one bereaved mother. Traumatic deaths have a way of being repulsive.

In such gruesome or repulsive events, people may not have known a particular person who died in the trauma, but they still feel a sense of loss. Exposure to gruesomeness carries its own sense of loss, the loss of decency, civility, and innocence. Still others may have not just observed gruesomeness but have participated in it or contributed to it. They feel "dirty" or stained by their involvement in the trauma. What might the experience of loss be in such circumstances?

The repulsive nature of some traumas or traumatic deaths makes it all the more difficult to come to terms with the loss. It is hard to get a hold of the experience of loss in circumstances that are so repulsive. The repulsiveness overwhelms and crowds out other emotions. Some people might feel both repulsion and great sadness.

Collective Losses

A collective loss is a loss that many people share and experience together at the same time, a loss that affects their sense of group identity, their communal life, and how the community functions. The "patient" here is the community, not the individual. Awareness of this kind of loss as a distinctive and unique kind of loss was crystallized in the minds of many by the terrorist attack on United States on September 11, 2001. Most Americans experienced a generalized sense of loss of something significant, even if they did not personally know any of the victims. Since then, Americans have experienced together the varied ways in which the trauma of 9/11 has rippled through our collective psyche, culture, and governmental functioning. It might be better to label 9/11 as a collective trauma rather than a collective loss. Most collective losses come upon a community, especially on the national level, in the form of trauma. Such national traumas almost always include the loss of life. Yet, within this larger trauma, there can also be various secondary losses: the loss of innocence, loss of security, and loss of pride.

Natural disasters are by their very nature experienced collectively. Tornados destroy entire towns; with`in each town there are individual traumas and individual losses, but there is also a loss experienced by the whole town collectively. In recent years, other natural disasters might also come to mind, such as hurricanes and fires that destroyed portions of United States in 2017 or the human-made traumatic losses associated with mass shootings. In an era of instant, mass communication, all of these national losses impact people even at a great physical distance from the trauma event.

Most ministers should be familiar with the concept of collective losses because congregations sometimes experience this type of loss. A collective loss may come in the form of the departure of a beloved minister. Or, such a loss may come in the form of the death of an installed pastor or of a significant emotional leader of the congregation. Sometimes the loss comes in the form of the gradual decline of the congregation through lower membership rolls, changing neighborhoods, or the assimilation of members from other cultures. Sometimes loss comes in the form of a congregation losing its sanctuary by fire, tornado, or some other natural disaster. Just like individuals and families, congregations experience significant collective losses.

The role and impact of losses in the life of a congregation is not a new concept to most religious leaders. Within the last twenty years or so, denominational officials have focused on this issue. In response, the specialized ministry of interim ministry has arisen in many denominations. Interim ministers assume leadership in a recently bereaved congregation and assist the congregation in processing their grief and making the necessary organizational adjustments. Religious administrators have learned, sometimes the hard way, that unless a congregation processes its communal grief, it cannot embrace a new pastor, new leadership, or new vision for its ministry.

> *The assassination of Martin Luther King Jr. was a collective trauma that affected America on many levels. Those closest to Martin lost a friend, a pastor, a confidant, and a leader. The movement lost a dream. African Americans lost a symbol. The church lost a prophet. America lost a Nobel Peace Prize laureate. What will the historians*

who write the story of our great nation say that America lost on that tragic day in April 1968? Certainly, many have worked to mitigate these losses, but they were nevertheless losses.

Every group, community, or system has a sense of itself, which is its collective identity, and of its collective purpose or mission. As noted above, the death of Martin Luther King Jr. was a loss to a variety of communities. All collective traumas or losses force the affected communities to do what individuals do in trauma recovery: manage their anxiety, share their trauma stories, and come to grips with their collective losses. Communities are also forced to review the group's sense of itself and its identity, core beliefs, values, and purpose. As do individuals, some communities or systems seem to double down on their pretrauma identity and purpose, whereas other communities refashion their identity and purpose to be more suitable for the posttrauma world.

Chronic Losses

The term "ambiguous losses" was popularized by Pauline Boss of the University of Minnesota in her book by the same name.[4] An ambiguous loss is a loss that is unclear and chronic. It is caused by no definite or single event. Boss argued that ambiguous losses are increasingly common in the modern world. She cited two types of ambiguous losses: leaving without goodbye and goodbye without leaving

An example of leaving without goodbye would be soldiers who are missing in action (MIAs). They are gone, but there is no closure, no final word on their fate, and no funeral. Their loved ones are left hanging in emotional limbo. Is the soldier dead or alive? There is no opportunity to say goodbye or to grieve because the loss is not finalized. There is no body and no burial. It is a trauma—a chronic trauma. Another example in this category is when a person (often a young person) disappears, is kidnapped, or runs away and their fate is not clear. Again, the family is left in emotional limbo until they receive some word on the whereabouts or fate of their loved one.

An example of goodbye without leaving would be the case of a person with Alzheimer's disease who gradually over time "leaves" (says goodbye) but is still present physically. Alzheimer's disease has become more

---

4. Boss, *Ambiguous Losses*.

common in modern times because people are living longer. It is now the sixth leading cause of death in the United States.[5] It is primarily a disease that causes a gradual decline of one's memory and related cognitive functioning. Family members who care for a loved one with Alzheimer's disease experience their beloved parent, grandparent, or spouse gradually declining to the point where they may literally forget who they are and/or cannot remember who their loved ones are. It is just heartbreaking! It is as if the person is not there anymore. Their identity, their spirit—their soul, if you will—is not there, and yet they have not left. They are still physically present. This loss is normally very gradual, persistent, and insidious. It is estimated that there are more than five million Americans living with Alzheimer's and that there are more than fifteen million unpaid caregivers.[6] Such people are in every congregation in America.

Sometimes the losses associated with trauma become chronic in nature. In a traumatic event, people can lose bodily functions or body parts, such as a leg, a breast, or a portion of their brain. These losses, while initially associated with an event, become more devastating over time. People must adapt and adjust, learning to compensate for their now lost function or body part. And in cases where a progressive disease is present, the loss may become more severe or more crippling over time. It is as if the trauma itself becomes drawn out, a chronic trauma.

Other examples may come to mind:

- a cancer patient who gradually declines over time;
- a developmentally disabled child who fails to develop normally and is there in body but not in mind;
- a wounded soldier who is permanently impaired physically or mentally;
- A person with a brain injury who is not their old self but is still there in body.

Modern medical science has done some wonderful things in the last sixty years. Many people who previously would have died much sooner can now live on in a partially handicapped or impaired condition. It is a

---

5. National Center for Health Statistics, "Leading Causes of Death," *Center for Disease Control and Prevention*, http://www.cdc.gov/nchs/fastats/leading-causes-of-death.htm.

6. Alzheimer's Association, "2017 Alzheimer's Disease Facts and Figures," www.alz.org/facts/.

wonderful thing, but the success of medical science has created new challenges emotionally, socially, and spiritually.

Disenfranchised Losses

Disenfranchised losses refer to losses that are socially disdained or stigmatized by the culture or community in which they occur. A related term, "disenfranchised grief," is grief that is not openly acknowledged, embraced, or ritualized by community leaders and institutions because the loss is stigmatized.[7] This makes it difficult for people grieving such losses to acknowledge them and talk openly about them and thereby to receive community support. When these losses are both traumatic and stigmatized, it is hard for the next of kin or bereaved parties to grieve openly. Such circumstances result in higher rates of unresolved, blocked, or complicated grief.

The first example that comes to mind, one that many ministers or lay caregivers encounter sooner or later, is death by suicide. Suicide is the tenth leading cause of death overall in the United States, claiming over 44,000 lives last year.[8] Suicide is traumatic for the next of kin. Bereavement due to suicide is colored and shaped not just by grief but also by the varied emotions that typically accompany trauma. In addition to sorrow, the bereaved family members often feel strong doses of guilt, anger, shame over their loved one's act of self-destruction, and possibly anxiety over the loved one's ultimate fate. Successful recovery in these cases involves the working through of all of these varied emotions.

Various Christian communities have a long history of treating suicide as the ultimate sin—as murder—or at least as a shameful event. In the past, for example, suicide victims did not even receive a proper funeral or burial. On the other hand, Christian communities normally have compassion for everyone who suffers, and understanding suicide victims as suffering mentally helps reduce the stigma felt by many because of how their loved one died. Clearly, views on suicide still vary widely from family to family, church to church, and culture to culture. If the larger surrounding community feels disdain toward suicide in general and toward those who "take the coward's way out," for example, then surely they will be less generous

---

7. This term was first coined by Kenneth J. Doka in his 1989 book *Disenfranchised Grief*.

8. National Institute of Mental Health, www.nimh.nih.gov/health/statistics/suicide/index.shtml.

in offering the bereaved family the support they need to heal. Cultural or religious disdain will make an already difficult loss even more challenging.

> When Jane's first child was born, she was elated, but over time a melancholy overcame her. She thought it was post-partum depression, but it lingered for months. She was delighted to see how attentive her mother was to this newborn, her first grandchild. In the weeks and months that followed, Mom delighted in her grandchild's every accomplishment. It was nice to see Mom so happy, so normal, after the earlier years. Jane wondered, though, if her mother remembered the first time Jane was pregnant, some fifteen years earlier, when she was a teenager, young, immature, and a bit wild. She had been date raped by an older man. Her mother arranged for Jane to abort the fetus. It all seems so long ago now, so foggy; everything was so secretive. Now, Jane wonders if Mom remembers the earlier time.... Jane certainly does. What would it have been like if this newborn had an older sister or brother? Would Mom have been so attentive to that child or so proud of her? There is a hole in Jane's soul that yearns to be healed, even amid the joy of a new life.

This vignette illustrates another common example of a disenfranchised loss: the loss of a pregnancy. Jane became pregnant out of wedlock when she was a teenager, and then she had an abortion. If Jane had had a miscarriage instead of an abortion, would it have been easier for Jane and her mother to speak about it over the years? After a miscarriage, Jane might have experienced several losses—a loss of hope, expectations, dreams, and identity. Miscarriage is an unappreciated and often discounted type of loss in its own right, but abortion incorporates a complexity of ambiguous feelings, often buried in shame and isolation. Many young women who chose to have an abortion have few people to talk with to process their feelings, which may run the gamut from shame to relief. Abortion is a highly charged and controversial subject in many Christian communities. Abortion is an example of a disenfranchised loss, a loss that cannot be openly acknowledged and grieved in many Christian communities or other cultures that treat the subject with anger and disgust.

The disease of HIV/AIDS and its successful treatment has also come a long way in recent years. Those with HIV/AIDS are less stigmatized than they once were, but there was a time in the 1980s and 1990s, and there still are places in the United States today, in which death by AIDS was and still is a disenfranchised loss. It is a loss that is difficult to talk about openly, and thus it is difficult to receive community support. Some cultures and some religious communities still understand HIV/AIDS to be primarily a disease of homosexual persons and therefore, in their minds, the consequence of sinful behavior. Deaths associated with this disease can be traumatic for the family.

People dealing with the trauma related to disenfranchised losses may not seek or receive generous support from their normal communities of support, which are their congregations, family, and friends. More likely, they find the support they need by participating in a specialized group or organization comprised of people with similar experiences.

Ministers need to recognize their own feelings of disdain and bias. If a minister has emotional, moral, or theological discomfort about certain disenfranchised losses, then maybe he or she is not the right person to provide pastoral support for people experiencing a particular disenfranchised loss. That is fine. But at the same time, if one of their congregants is bereaved over a disenfranchised loss, caring ministers should set aside whatever theological or moral opinions they might have about the issue at hand and go to their congregant with compassion, empathy, and support. Ministers are not called to be guardians of moral purity but to offer the compassion and mercy of Jesus Christ.

Developmental Losses

Johnny was always an active, physical guy. He enjoyed sports and his busy job as a UPS driver. In his mid-forties Johnny was in a very serious motor vehicle crash. He nearly lost his life, and he had multiple severe injuries to his back and legs. After nearly two weeks in intensive care, he stabilized and improved. In time, he was released from the hospital and transferred to a rehab facility, where he began the long process of learning to stand and walk again. The rehab was slow, in spite of Johnny's positive can-do attitude. After using up his sick time and vacation time, Johnny was placed on state disability. After 125 days, the disability payments ran out. Alice, his spouse, dropped her volunteer work and increased her work hours. Miranda, his oldest daughter, dropped out of college and went to work. Doctors are now saying that Johnny will never be able to walk normally again. Based on this verdict, his employer recently suggested that Johnny take early retirement. When their priest comes by for his regular visit, Johnny, who is not prone to expressing his emotions, begins to cry. "I guess I am not going back to work, Father."

Losses

He reaches for the priest's hand. "Father, how can I do this retirement thing at my age? Is there a ritual or something?"

When losses occur at a key turning point in one's life cycle and those losses are fairly predictable, inevitable, and somewhat common to others at the same stage in life, they are considered developmental losses. This term stands in contrast to accidental losses, which are random, unpredictable, not inevitable, and often unique to the participant. Another word for accidental losses might be traumatic losses. The distinction between developmental and accidental losses is based on timing, predictability, and universality. The death of one's parents in the fullness of years is a developmental loss for most people, whereas the death of one's child is typically an accidental loss.

In the above vignette, Johnny's loss begins as an accidental loss, a tragic and traumatic event, but over time it becomes clear that it is also a developmental loss, a loss that ushers in a new stage of life, one that is atypical. Johnny's struggle is to make that shift, to realize that he cannot go back to his pretrauma life but must move on to a new stage of his life. Developmental losses are understood as necessary losses. People must let go of the past in order to move on to the next stage of life. If they hang on emotionally to a deceased spouse, they are prevented from moving on to the next stage, the post-marriage stage of life. Newly discharged soldiers must let go of military life before they can reenter civilian society. Johnny must let go of his attachment to his previous job and all related aspects before he can embrace his new stage of life as a retired or second-career person. Generally speaking, people must say goodbye to the past before they can welcome the future.

Most of the upsetting losses in life are accidental losses, losses that are not chosen, are not universal, and are by definition unpredictable. The possible gains are hard to imagine. The tragic death of a person's mother when the child was twelve years old is a difficult loss to mourn, and it is certainly one in which the "gain" is not immediately clear. An unwelcome dismissal from a prized job could also be difficult to accept. If one is brutally assaulted, the several significant embedded losses overshadow and trivialize any silver lining.

However, accidental losses can also be developmental in the sense that they trigger a psychosocial transition, as illustrated in the above vignette. Not all of the transitions of adult life are universal or predictable. A given psychosocial transition may represent a detour compared to the common sequence of human life stages, but life is filled with detours. Everyone has his or her own unique path through adulthood. So, in a sense, every traumatic loss is a developmental loss and inevitably ushers in a new stage of one's life.

Loss as Breaking Emotional Bonds

Loss is the result of something both external and internal, something both objective and subjective. Objectively, loss is a loss because something has changed, because something in the real world is different: a person has died, a town has been destroyed, a bomb has exploded, or a person has been attacked. Subjectively, loss is also a function of something internal, something emotional. That something is the emotional bond a person has with what is lost. If there is no emotional bond, there is no loss. There is only change, even trauma, but no loss. The experience of loss is a result of change (external) and emotional bonding (internal).

Viewing loss as a function of the breaking of an emotional bond is rooted in attachment theory, which is associated with British psychiatrist John Bowlby, a pioneer in the early study of grief.[9] Humans naturally and universally form emotional bonds with loved ones and close friends. This instinct to attach has its genesis in the first year of life, when infants and primary caregivers normally establish a powerful and formative bond. When that bond is severed or broken, grief occurs. Based on his studies of infant attachment, Bowlby divided bereavement into four phases.

1. Initially, the griever experiences *numbing*, which is the feeling of being stunned and unable to process information.
2. The next phase is *yearning and searching*, which is a combination of intense separation anxiety and "defensive exclusion" that triggers the desire to search for and recover what is lost.
3. Repeatedly failing to find what is lost leads to *disorganization and despair*.
4. This is followed by *reorganization*.

Although attachment instincts have their origin in early human development, humans clearly form emotional bonds that extend beyond family members much more broadly and universally. People form emotional bonds with pets, possessions, jobs, places, sports teams, and even ideologies.

9. This model of grief is summarized nicely in Parkes, *Love and Loss*, 10–12.

Humans are social-emotional creatures who naturally, inevitably, form emotional bonds. It is always a bit amazing to me that in the course of a feature-length movie, moviegoers can form such a strong emotional bond with the main character that some cry like babies at the drama's tragic end . . . after just two hours! For most people, this bonding is automatic and inevitable. Familiarity breeds attachment. When these bonds are broken, we experience loss.

This understanding of loss as a function of attachment is embraced by Kenneth Mitchell and Herbert Anderson in their book *All Our Losses, All Our Griefs*. They begin their 1983 classic with the proposition that loss is a broader category than death, that "loss, not death, is the normative metaphor for understanding those experiences in human life that produce grief."[10] By carefully classifying the various types of loss, Mitchell and Anderson have helped an entire generation of ministers and Christian caregivers see the full array of potential losses and thus of possible griefs. Caregivers never know for sure what a person's strongest emotional bonds are. Maybe none of us knows the full range of our own bonds, either, not until they are severed. What do we cherish most in our lives? Sometimes we do not know until we lose it.

Grief counselors often share these comforting words: "Grief is where love was." Or, to paraphrase, grief is the form love takes when someone we loved dies. One cannot lose something if one never possessed it emotionally. Yet, upon reflection, this truism maybe a bit simplistic, however comforting it may be. Mary Ainsworth, a second-generation researcher on attachment theory, focused on the character of the attachment bond, not just on the strength of the bond.[11] She and her associates were able to identify various types or styles of emotional attachment, again largely by focusing, as Bowlby did, on the relationships between infants and their mothers. She identified two main patterns of attachment:

1. secure attachment
2. insecure attachment (anxious/ambivalent, avoidant, or disorganized/disoriented)

Ainsworth's work suggests that not all emotional bonds are the same and that the strength of the emotional bond alone is not always the best predictor of the experience of loss and thus of grief. People who have largely

---

10. Mitchell and Anderson, *All Our Losses, All Our Griefs*, 19.
11. Mary Ainsworth's work is also summarized in Parkes, *Love and Loss*, 13–16.

avoided forming significant emotional attachments may not experience a sense of loss. People who have an insecure pattern of attachment often experience an ambiguous or conflicted sense of loss, e.g., "I am both sad and relieved." Although attachment styles are formed in the earliest years of life, attachment theorists argue that people's attachment and detachment styles are repeated and reinforced throughout their adult lives.

Ainsworth's work and attachment theory in general suggests that the experience of loss is more complex and ambiguous than most people might imagine. Loss is a function of the relationship, not just the event. Picking up on this insight, Mitchell and Anderson address this in their definition of grief as the "response to a significant loss, intensified and complicated by the relationship to the person or the object lost."[12] If emotional bonds were always pure and strong, it would be easy to predict which potential losses people might find most threatening or most upsetting when they are ruptured. Yet, humans are complex creatures. The severity of a particular loss is determined by the intensity and complexity of the emotional bond with what has been lost.

Viewing loss through the lens of attachment theory reaffirms that each person lives in a web of attachments, some strong, some weak, some conflicted, and some ambiguous. Ministers and caregivers really cannot predict how people will experience a loss based on the external event. Loss is a function of the complex, messy, and yet universal human instinct to emotionally attach.

Anxiety and Grieving

Trauma evokes fear. Loss evokes grief. These are different dynamics, but the overlapping element is threat. Both trauma and loss are threats to one degree or another (see figure 3). Anxiety is thus common to both trauma and loss, and it is especially strong in traumatic loss. Yet, anxiety is a state and grief is a process. Severe or chronic anxiety can thus contaminate or even block grieving.

---

12. Mitchell and Anderson, *All Our Losses, All Our Griefs*, 54.

Figure 3
Trauma and Loss

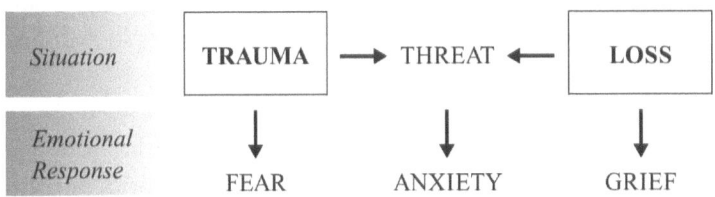

In some cases, the loss or losses are so obvious and immediate that people are thrown into an intense form of grief that is now referred to as traumatic grief. Traumatic grief is a mixture that is composed of more anxiety than grief, and it can look more like panic than sorrow. It is a time of intense stress. Usually, as the threat dissipates, as social support and resources fall into place, and as the trauma story becomes clear, traumatic grief tends to give way to "regular" grief. In other words, anxiety gives way to grief.

In other traumas in which the losses are not as immediate or obvious and fear is the prevalent dynamic, people tend to invoke various defense mechanisms to cope with their emotions: denial, avoidance, idealization, regression, delay, and even revenge. Such mechanisms prevent people from recognizing their losses. That's okay, up to a point. If people are recovering medically, they may need to be strong, to maintain hope. They may need to not give in to their sorrow while they are fighting to recover. It might be better for them to wait to try to comprehend the full scope of their loss (or losses) until they are medically whole or at least partially whole. Fear and intense, chronic anxiety work to prevent people from even seeing their losses. They are focused just on the threat. Only as the anxiety becomes manageable or dissipates do people begin to recognize the full scope of what they have lost and then enter into a grief process.

For people recovering from a prolonged trauma, anxiety is especially troublesome because anxiety has become ingrained over time in their psychological structures. In the early phases of recovery work, exploring the complexities of the embedded losses in their trauma only increases their anxiety. Moving too fast to acknowledge their losses can lead people to be retraumatized. Thus it is very important that such people be in safe places, have a trusting relationship with a therapist, and learn to manage their anxieties before they explore the full scope and complexities of what they have lost. Grief work is really not fully possible until the losses are recognized, and the losses cannot be recognized as long as the anxiety is intense and overwhelming. Of course, people do cry when they are overwhelmed or even when they are scared, but the deep, sorrowful tears must wait until the threat dissipates. Only after the fear subsides do people then begin to see what they have lost.

Neuroscientists describe the human brain as actually "three brains" or three neurological systems. These are the reptilian brain or reactive brain, the mammalian or limbic brain, and the cerebral cortex or reasoning brain, sometimes referred to as the doing brain, feeling brain, and thinking brain. Intense, life-threatening situations triggered by trauma first activate the reptilian brain, with its fight-or-flight response. Realizing the loss of a loved one then activates a grief response, associated with the limbic brain. The mammalian brain is focused on emotional bonding and connecting with loved ones. Actually, it is not that simple. Threat also activates the mammalian brain in order to mobilize people to connect with others for safety, and, in turn, the loss of a loved one can also be experienced as a threat at some level to the reptilian brain and trigger strong fears. There is some overlap. Even so, the distinction between the foci of the reptilian and mammalian brains, however simplified, is helpful. This leads me to say boldly that trauma hijacks bereavement! Trauma activates the threat response system of the reptilian brain. Fear floods the mind. The cerebral cortex copes by throwing up psychological defenses and various coping mechanisms—denial, justification, dissociation, intellectualization, numbing, and even revenge—all in a vain attempt to cope with the threat. These may all be necessary, but the price one pays is the inability to feel or to allow oneself to feel vulnerable, which is the doorway to grieving. Severe anxiety tends to block grief work, to block activation of the limbic system. Chronic anxiety similarly tends to inhibit tears.

After the trauma dissipates, or when people feel safe or have learned to manage their anxieties better, most people let their defenses down. They become more open to recognizing their losses and entering grief work. Alas, some people do not. In effect, PTSD can be understood as a maintaining of the threat response well after the threat is gone. It is a sustaining of the self-reinforcing dynamics of fear and anxiety on a continuing basis. It is a deepening and generalizing of the brain's fear-based neuropathways. And, the occasional triggers that reactivate anxiety or lead to significant retraumatization only reinforce the threat response. The lingering residue of trauma, chronic anxiety, keeps people from entering into the healing process of grief.

For most people, those who are generally successful in their recovery and healing, the mechanism for moving from anxiety to grief is remembering and storying. As people remember and share their trauma story, they come to recognize their losses, large and small, obvious and subtle, and as they embrace these losses, they naturally move further into sorrow.

The grief that follows a significant trauma is not always smooth or linear. Anxiety and grief are more like two interwoven threads on a quilt. Generally, though, as anxiety fades, the grieving process is allowed to proceed and to move one into mourning what has been lost. In becoming more open to one's losses, one becomes more vulnerable and thus more open to receiving support from others and from a compassionate God. God draws close to the wounded heart, not the hardened heart.

Public Rituals around Traumatic Loss

Public rituals can help people recognize loss and thus facilitate grief. Grief is lessened when it is shared. In fact, people grieve better when they participate in public rituals. The primary public ritual associated with a traumatic loss is the funeral or memorial services. When death or losses are traumatic in flavor, the interplay between anxiety and grief is striking.

The traditional funeral or memorial service is a rite fashioned to help people grieve. The gathered community provides a safe and supportive environment where people can express their emotions. Music, prayers, and even photographs of the deceased are designed to evoke grieving. If the body of the deceased is present, the viewing ritual is similarly designed to evoke grief and bring closure. Eulogies help people remember, to form stories and memories of the deceased, thus facilitating the grief work. The subsequent burial helps mourners bring the process to some closure.

When the death is caused by a trauma, the funeral or memorial service carries the additional emotional weight of the trauma as well as the loss. In the aftermath of a trauma or traumatic death, the gathered congregation in a funeral service may still be in shock. Anxiety fills the room. People have many questions. How did this happen? How did it happen so fast? Did the deceased suffer? Could it happen to me? Are we safe now? The aim of the ritual becomes not just to help people grieve but also to help them feel safe. In the aftermath of a traumatic death, as noted in the previous chapter, family and friends are focused on how their loved one died rather than on the merits of his or her life. They want and need to know the trauma story. However, there is usually an absence of information, a lack of an explanation or consensus story about what this death means. Or, more likely, the funeral or memorial service must serve people with multiple stories or perspectives about what this particular death means. This multiplicity of stories is especially apparent if the traumatic death is a public trauma or a controversial loss, i.e., a disenfranchised loss.

Funeral or memorial services that occur in the aftermath of a trauma have to balance two needs: the need for safety and explanations of what happened vs. the more traditional focus on the life of the deceased and the facilitation of grief. The challenge of the minister is to "read the room" accurately. Are the needs of the assembled mourners more for safety, reassurance, and stability or for remembering and grieving what is lost? Most of the time, it is some of both, and the main difference is the relative portions of each. The funeral or memorial service will be beneficial if it can help people recognize the loss or losses embedded in the trauma event and move, ever so gently, from trauma recovery work to grief work. Mature ministers craft a service that moves from a focus on anxiety to a focus on grief, helping people move through shock to grief, from trauma stories to stories about a life well lived.

Conclusion

This chapter has explored the many forms and ways that loss is a part of or is triggered by trauma, suggesting that loss is more prevalent and complex than most people might realize. Although there are great variations among people and types of trauma, I have suggested that trauma recovery gives way to bereavement as anxiety dissipates and a fuller realization of the loss occurs. It is not a smooth, linear, or easy process. Some start grieving immediately at the moment of trauma, whereas others must feel safe, stabilize their lives, and manage their anxiety before they can explore what they have lost and enter into grieving.

Ministers and other caregivers can play an important role in helping people through this transition. By listening carefully and reflecting back what they hear, caregivers can help traumatized people become bereaved people. Caregivers who themselves are comfortable with their own vulnerabilities, hurts, wounds, and losses are best able to help others see and appreciate what they have lost.

Through embracing their losses, people are able to move past trauma to a new stage in their journey toward wholeness. Letting go of threat and embracing loss also softens people's hearts, making them more open, more vulnerable, and more compassionate. Vulnerable people are more open to receiving mercy and comfort, both from others and from a compassionate God. Recovery naturally flows into bereavement. Chapter 4 addresses the next phase, the grief process.

Questions for Personal Reflection

1. What is the most significant loss in your life to date?
2. Of the various types of losses discussed in this chapter, which one(s) have you or your immediate family experienced?
3. Many denominations regularly relocate their clergy. What kinds of potential losses might be involved in such a transition? How might the regularity of such losses affect a minister?
4. What kinds of losses might the parents of a disabled child experience? Describe several examples of possible losses.
5. What might the grief symptoms from a loss of faith look like?
6. Research the term "rite of passage" in the anthropological literature on rituals.
7. What are the disenfranchised losses in your religious community?
8. Give some examples of secondary losses that may arise as a consequence of a primary loss.
9. Go online and research the incidence of substance abuse among traumatized or bereaved persons. What other kinds of compulsive behaviors do people employ to cope with trauma or loss?
10. Have you officiated at a funeral or memorial service for a person whose death was particularly traumatic? How are the dynamics of such rituals different from a death that is anticipated and is nontraumatic?

4

Grief

As losses are acknowledged, traumatized people become bereaved people. Grief is the normal and universal emotional response to a perceived loss. Studies of universal human facial expressions by Paul Ekman and associates have identified sorrow as one of the six basic human emotions.[1] Regardless of culture, gender, age, or race, we all recognize the human facial expression of someone in grief. This facial expression is universal because the emotion of grief is universal. Indeed, we all have tear ducts. Each and every human is created to cry. Ultimately, none of us are meant to be "tough guys." Those tear ducts are there for a reason. Crying is part and parcel of our human makeup. We might even say that God wants us to cry. Grief is good.

In this chapter, I explore the dynamics of grief to help ministers and other spiritual caregivers understand what makes for successful grief work and thereby be better able to offer support and serve as ritual leaders and spiritual guides to the bereaved. I begin this exploration of grief by noting that grief is as much a verb as it is a noun. Grieving is dynamic, not static. Grieving is always in motion. It has energy. It has a telos; it is directional. Pioneer grief scholar Colin Murray Parkes writes that "grief is a *process* of realization, of 'making real' the fact of the loss."[2] As much as it might appear to be past oriented, it is really future oriented. In contrast to PTSD, which keeps people fixated on the past, grief carries people into the future. Grieving pushes people toward healing. If grieving is suppressed or delayed, it

---

1. Ekman and Friesen, *Unmasking the Face*.
2. Parkes, *Bereavement*, 156.

cries out for expression and completion. Grieving can be delayed, of course, but grief can never be eliminated or avoided. Grief longs for expression.

Grieving is also a natural process. It is a normal response to loss. It is not a mental illness, although it certainly can trigger or reactivate a psychological disorder. Normal grief, or bereavement without trauma, is a natural human process. Grief is as inevitable and universal as the human impulse to love and cherish one another.

The Process Begins

Grieving is a process set in motion by a loss, even a perceived or anticipated loss. The early phases of this process are often acute when the loss is shocking or traumatic in some way. In such circumstances, people are overwhelmed with intense grieving, grief that comes over them in waves that last anywhere from minutes to a full hour with accompanying somatic distress and symptoms. Acute grief is all-consuming; it is a demanding companion. Relief is found only in the assurance that, over time, grief's intensity will lessen. Acute grief is time-limited. It tends to peak within days or a week of the loss event. Over time, people cry less often and less intensely, until finally the tears are only occasional.

Grieving ebbs and flows like the tides. Just as we cannot jump into a hot bathtub all at once, the bereaved must take the new painful reality in doses. The most common and effective kind of grief dynamic is one that oscillates between release and structure, like waves interspaced with periods of rest—not too much avoidance and not too much emotional release. Too much avoidance or too much release is not as helpful as the alternating approach. One cannot and should not cry all the time, nor should one suppress one's tears all the time.

The expression of grief is shaped by culture, family norms, and personality. Some people express grief rather easily and intensely; others prefer to express their pain in private or with restraint. Generally speaking, most people do not give as much license to their grief as they could. They tend to shut it off prematurely out of fear that its intensity will overwhelm them or they will never stop crying. They fear that the intensity alone will make them crazy. Generally speaking, however, the more people give voice to their grief, the more easily they will pass through it.

Grief must be passed through. "The only way out is through," as wise bereavement counselors say. In this sense, grieving is like birthing. Once birthing starts, the only way out is through. And, similar to giving birth, successful grieving involves a lot of work, which is why it is called grief *work*.

Grief's Phases

Because grief is clearly a process and because grieving clearly changes over time, it is tempting for caregivers to identify "stages" of grief work. It is comforting to bereaved people to be reassured that they are in the "anger stage" or the middle stages. Stage talk gives a sense of normalization that most people in acute grief need. In the early years of grief studies, many well-meaning writers therefore offered lists of grief's stages. Most of the longer lists included shock, disbelief, tears, physical distress, anger, depression, guilt, loneliness, and confusion, followed by reintegration.[3] The current thinking is that there are no clear, universal stages in major bereavement. The elements of grieving vary widely according to the nature of the loss, family and cultural norms, and the individual's unique temperamental and psychological history. Furthermore, the grief process appears to be more spiral than linear. People tend to experience the various "stages" of the grief process repetitively in slightly different forms.[4] As C. S. Lewis once noted regarding his own spousal grief, "Nothing stays put."[5] So, over time, the longer lists of stages have given way to more generalized three- or four-stage schemas, such as acute grief, disorientation/withdrawal, and reorganization/integration (see figure 4).

---

3. One of the most popular books on pastoral care is Granger E. Westberg's *Good Grief* (originally published in 1962), which has been recently republished. Westberg lists ten stages of grief.

4. Grief is often represented graphically as a wheel or grief cycle.

5. Lewis, *A Grief Observed*, 46.

Grief

Figure 4
Phases of Grief

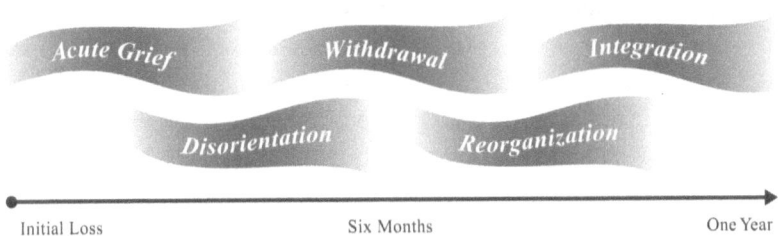

If the loss is gradual, anticipatory grieving is the prequel or the first stage of grief work. Conversely, if the loss is a surprise, shock or numbness is the first phase of grief work. If the shock is intense and the loss is horrific and unexpected, the preferred term is *trauma*. If the loss is embedded in trauma, then trauma symptoms and grief work get all mixed up. The trauma recovery process and the grief work become parallel and interwoven processes. Usually, the reduction of trauma symptoms becomes the first and most pressing focus of the healing process. Trauma recovery is not complete without grief work because the losses associated with trauma are often more pervasive and important that initially realized. The grief work (and growth work) may need to go on for years even after the trauma symptoms have been managed.

Grief's Companions

In addition to its process character, grief can also be confusing because of the array of other emotions that can accompany grief work. Grieving or the grief process does not consist of any one single emotion. It is a collection of emotions whose presence and relative intensity varies from person to person. A grieving person may bounce around from one emotion to another. If nothing else, grieving is characterized by emotional instability. These are some of the emotions that may surface in the course of grieving:

- *Emptiness and longing.* At its core, grief is experienced as a sense of emptiness, a sadness that something or someone dear is gone. It is a yearning, a longing or pining for what is lost. This is typically expressed as sadness and crying. Sadness is the core and continuous thread throughout the grieving process.

- *Anger and hostility.* Bereaved people can be irritable, easily upset, and crabby. Protest is a part of grief, especially if the loss is perceived as unfair, unjust, or unexpected. Anger can be easily displaced, so hostility can come out at a variety of targets, including the deceased, caregivers, loved ones, doctors, or God. As with grief itself, the outward expression of anger is influenced by family and cultural norms. Anger can be an intense emotion. Anger can also go underground, leading to chronic resentment or contributing to depression.

- *Helplessness and powerlessness.* When people experience a loss, especially the death of a loved one, they experience a power larger than themselves determining their life. They are not in control. They are mere creatures, standing in awe of the mysteries of life and death. If the loss came embedded in trauma, then this sense of helplessness is accentuated. Helplessness feeds into and reinforces depression. In some ways, venting anger in bereavement actually helps one reclaim one's power and agency and stay out of the pit of despair.

- *Relief and freedom.* On the opposite end of the scale from anger, bereaved people may also feel relief or a sense of freedom in the context of a significant loss. If the loved one suffered a long time, their death can come as a relief, a relief for the deceased and a relief for the next of kin who carried the burden of their care for many years. Or, if people suffered through an unhappy or abusive relationship, then the death of that relationship will bring a new sense of freedom and optimism for the future. Sometimes relief also comes toward the end of ordinary bereavement as a sign of its completion. As the grief is worked through, bereaved people may realize, even in a mystical way, that their loved one is at peace, and with that realization comes relief. Or perhaps, with the passage of time, people look back on what was lost with a new perspective, realizing they are better off now than they were before. Relief can come in several forms.

- *Guilt and shame.* As the bereaved reflect upon their loss, feelings of guilt and/or shame can arise. It is quite common for the bereaved to dwell on what they could have done or should not have done, what they wish they had said or not said. They assume a greater sense of personal responsibility for the loss than is realistic. Children are especially vulnerable to concluding that they are responsible for a death in the family. Guilt can also be intensified by the circumstances of the loss, such as when a person had to make a difficult decision that led to the death of their loved one, initiated the decision that dissolved their marriage, or made an instant choice between saving their own life or the lives of their fellow soldiers. Guilt can be intensified for people who are more prone to be self-incriminating. Regardless of these variables, almost everyone who is involved in a significant loss has to sort out their relative degree of responsibility for the loss. Whose fault was it, and to what degree was it their fault? Shame is similar to guilt but is not the same. Feelings of shame or embarrassment arise when the bereaved believe that the loss or the expression of grief itself is a sign of weakness or moral failure. Shame is often present in the case of disenfranchised losses, as noted in the previous chapter. In some cultural contexts, some losses or the situations surrounding the losses are so reprehensible that the community does not encourage grief or offer social support.

- *Depression and withdrawal.* Bereaved people often experience a depressive mood as a part of or concurrent to their grief. A depressive mood is characterized by feelings of hopelessness, futility, self-pity, and/or a sense of diminishment due to the loss event. These depressive episodes can lead people to withdraw from others and from activities and interests that used to give them pleasure. They may stop or have trouble keeping up with their normal routine and personal habits such as housekeeping, self-care, work, and social obligations. The severity and character of these depressive moods vary according to the person, their mental health history, and the nature of the loss. Usually, the depression associated with bereavement, whatever its severity, is transient. It is something people pass through. The time of the greatest vulnerability to a struggle with depression is in the middle phases of bereavement, after the funeral is over and the emergency social supports have faded away. For some people, especially those with a history of depression prior to the loss event, bereavement can trigger or cause a relapse of clinical depression, depression that is chronic, persistent, and severe.

- *Fear and anxiety.* When the loss or death of a loved one comes embedded in trauma, the trauma-related fears carry over into the grief work as anxiety. Most notably, traumatized people worry that something similar will happen again to them or to someone they love. Traumatic grief includes intense anxiety, and that intense anxiety, if not managed or reduced, can actually block bereavement, as I discussed in the previous chapter. Some anxiety, however, is a normal part of the grief process, even in nontraumatic losses. Any significant loss is a major change event, and until the future gets sorted out, life can feel uncertain and in limbo. Furthermore, for people who have a predisposition to anxiety and/or who are unusually dependent, their pre-loss or pre-trauma fears and insecurities will be intensified by their loss. Their bereavement will be colored by or even dominated by their chronic worries or even occasional panic attacks, drowning out any recognition of grief per se. Such people will exhibit more controlling, obsessive, or compulsive behaviors during bereavement. Whatever the source of the anxiety, anxiety management techniques will be an important part of, maybe even a prerequisite to, grief work, as they are for trauma recovery work.

These are some of the main players in the grief process, the emotions that "ride along in the grief posse." Their presence and intensity color the grief process. For purposes of discussion, I have delineated these various emotions, but in reality, grief feelings are seldom distinct. They get all mixed up. The grief process is a "tear soup," as a book by the same name suggests.[6] Each person's recipe for tear soup is a unique mixture of ingredients. The tear soup of some people can have heavy doses of anger, shame, or anxiety, so much so that one would hardly recognize the soup as bereavement. Others' tear soup consists of a mixture of apparently contradictory feelings. In fact, I would suggest that 90 percent of the time, the dynamics of grieving are best characterized as ambivalent feelings: love-hate, relief-fear, sorrow-guilt. Even the purest of losses have elements of ambivalence and changeability. Furthermore, individual variables color the process, too. People with limited verbal skills, for example, tend to act out their grief rather than talk it out. People inclined to be aggressive, depressed, or dependent give their tear soup those distinctive flavors. And, of course, age is an important variable, too. Children express their pain in ways that may not look like grief to adults, and I suspect that elderly people manifest their grief differently than middle-aged people. For purposes of discussion, I have delineated the various emotional elements that accompany grief, but, in reality, each

---

6. Schwiebert and DeKlyen, *Tear Soup*.

person's recipe for tear soup is unique, shaped by the circumstances of the loss, the character of the attachment, the personality of the bereaved, and the availability of social support and resources. The emotions associated with grieving are varied, changeable, and complicated because life and love and attachment are like that—changeable, complicated, and ambivalent. Ministers and other caregivers can be most supportive when they honor the varied ambiguities and emotional diversity of grief work.

How Long Does Grieving Take?

There is no fixed timetable for grief to do its work. Some people move through their grief in short order, others seem to be on a slow boat, and still others seem to get detoured here and there, thus prolonging their journey. Generally, the rule of thumb is that most significant losses take about one year to fully adjust to. A full year allows the bereaved to pass through all of the anniversaries once. In earlier times, there were prescribed mourning periods that encouraged people to give it a full year in order to see the process through to its completion. Modern people tend to shun prescribed rituals and traditional customs in this regard. If anything, most modern people rush through bereavement. Encouraging people to be patient with their sorrow and to "steady the course" is always good guidance for the bereaved.

Does grief ever really end? For most people and most losses, grief does end, at least the acute phase of grief. Yet, for some significant losses, like the tragic death of a loved one, the sorrow may never really go away. The grieving may end, but the sorrow can linger for a lifetime, prompting the saying, "For most people grief does end, but loss is forever." Or to paraphrase, for significant losses people do not get over grief as much as they integrate it. Especially for older people or people with a series of losses, it might be said that people learn to live with grief rather than get over it, as the title of Dorothy Becvar's book *In the Presence of Grief* suggests. Most people never completely forget or stop missing someone dear to them. They move on, not so much leaving behind their sorrows as incorporating them into a stronger, more complex soul. We do not completely lose someone dear to us so much as we internalize the relationship. Or, to frame it differently, there is a "continuing bond" with our loved one, an emotional bond that transcends the death.⁷ Maybe love does not end so much as it changes, as the Scriptures teach.

The Healing Process

Melissa M. Kelley, in *Grief: Contemporary Theory and the Practice of Ministry*, proposes that grief is a mosaic of processes and dynamics—a rich tapestry of layers, colors, and textures that are woven together into grief.⁸ Indeed, a review of the various emotions that accompany grief, its dynamic character, and its idiosyncratic nature, based on the person affected, makes mosaic an apt metaphor. However, I still think that it is possible to identify the elements of a generalized process. Or, to put it another way, what does the grief process look like apart from trauma? Or, what are the conditions that facilitate healing? Here is my description of the pure, uncomplicated grief process and the essential components of healing.

The Value of Tears

The single most important factor in the healing process is the full and free expression of emotions. Crying helps . . . a lot. Crying releases pent-up emotions. Crying releases what is termed in trauma studies the "freeze response." It's cathartic. Crying gives voice to the pain. The expression of crying, particularly weeping in public, varies. Some people cry a lot, almost nonstop. Others cry very little. Some people express their pain indirectly, such as through dancing, painting, writing, or making music. Everyone needs to cry, and, generally speaking, the more crying, the better. Probably, if anything, people do not cry enough.

> Rogelio's son got involved in a local gang and was arrested several times, and he regularly used drugs. He was shot and killed in a drive-by shooting. It was a horrible time for Rogelio. He did not cry much, but over the weeks and months to follow, he became irritable and grouchy. He was consumed with anger toward the gangs, toward the gang-affiliated families, and toward himself. He asked, "How could this have happened to our family? Where did we go wrong?" He had always been a stern law-and-order guy, and he thought he had set a clear standard for his son. Two months later, he got into

---

7. I borrow the term *continuing bond* from Klass et al., eds., *Continuing Bonds*.
8. See Kelley, *Grief*.

> an argument with a neighborhood father, whose son was a noted runner. Rogelio was nearly arrested for assault. His priest pleaded with him to attend a local meeting of Compassionate Friends, a support group for parents of murdered children. Rogelio remembers the day of his first meeting very well; it was the day he let go, the day he sobbed like a baby, the day he accepted the tragic loss of his only son. It was the day, he says years later, that he really lost his son and began to find himself again.

Although the expression of all of the feelings people experience in connection with a loss is cathartic, anger is a tricky emotion to regulate internally and to manage socially. Too much anger or inappropriate anger can cause more harm than healing. To rephrase it, anger, or, more precisely, hatred, can disguise and block grief. Anger and the desire for revenge, as I suggest in a subsequent chapter, can be a way of avoiding tears. A vengeful mind-set is a vain attempt to maintain control in the face of terrifying vulnerability. So, the full and free expression of emotions always needs to be balanced with and tempered by verbalization.

Talking Helps

The second important factor in the healing process is talking—verbalizing one's inner life. Putting feelings into words is a uniquely human trait. Humans are created for language and by language. Language helps us release our emotions. It helps us identify and label our feelings. Thus, it helps us recognize and acknowledge our feelings. It helps give some structure and order to our emotions so they do not overwhelm us. Words objectify our emotions as well as release them, thus giving us both freedom and structure. Words transform our suffering into something manageable.

> Prison chaplain Bonnie Jones runs a weekly trauma recovery support group for male lifers. "These fellows are a hardened bunch," she notes. "They are hardened for a good reason. Most of them have seen some pretty traumatic stuff, a few of them quite early in their lives. It is difficult to get them to talk about those deep wounds. Most of them are quite skilled, even without alcohol and drugs, at masking their vulnerabilities. And yet, they keep coming to group (it is voluntary), and in time—they have plenty of time—they open up and talk. I suppose I am the mother they never had . . . or something. A little piece of healing under a big umbrella of sadness."

Verbalizing and grieving go hand in hand. Bereaved people talk a lot, as well they should. People who do not talk much, who have poor verbal skills, who are overly well defended, or who are quite introverted, as most of Chaplain Bonnie's men are, often have a much harder time with grief work. This is why depression, which is a common element of the grief process, can be so dangerous. Depressed people often cease talking. They tend to turn inward rather than outward. That turn inward in effect stops the healing process. Sometimes the barriers to verbalization can be overcome through indirect means, such as by inviting people to journal, draw or paint, or even dance, but these indirect methods are effective only if they lead to words.

Empathy Heals

Talking implies that there is someone to listen, which brings us to another variable in the healing process. Bereaved people need to have someone to talk to, someone who can genuinely listen. The most healing kind of listening is empathetic listening, listening that is nonjudgmental, genuine, accurate, and fully attentive. Not everyone is able or willing to listen in this way to hurting loved ones or friends. Genuine listening is in short supply in this modern, impatient, and self-absorbed world. Genuine listening requires presence, being in the room and not preoccupied with other thoughts. Genuine listening requires patience because bereaved persons often repeat the same stories over and over as they gradually come to terms with what happened. Genuine listening is not just passive listening but listening in a way that encourages conversation and thus facilitates deeper sharing and, ultimately, deeper healing. Genuine listening and genuine sharing are mutually reinforcing. Together, they create open and authentic communication, a touching of minds, hearts, and souls. The caregiver and the care receiver connect and, in that experience of connection, healing begins. In short, empathy heals.

> *The grief support group always closed its weekly meetings with a group hug. For Jeanette, that was the best part of the program, just a moment, however brief, of tangible connection and support. These people understand me, she thought. My husband does not want to talk about it anymore, and most of my friends don't know what to say or wish I would get over it. The group was just for parents who had lost children via suicide. Jeanette's daughter had died of an*

> *overdose of illegal drugs three years earlier. These people understood the nagging guilt, the shame, and her torturous imagination of the final hours or their final conversation. These people understood all that, but the best part of the day was the hug.*

If empathy heals, then the best caregivers are listeners who are naturally empathetic. Friends and family can be empathetic, certainly, but it is hard to be fully and consistently empathetic if one has not suffered similarly. It takes training and patience. Sometimes, it is easier for the bereaved to experience empathy in the context of "people who have been there." Grief support groups are ideal because fellow grief sufferers usually have the time, compassion, and empathy to be fully present with one another. Fellow grief sufferers know what it is like. They have a way of reading others, of knowing what hurting people are feeling even when they do not say anything, and thus are able to draw it out of them. Grief support groups provide the social support necessary for the bereaved to face the pain of their loss. Furthermore, the self-help format reinforces the normalcy of grief and the principle of mutuality, the idea that "we are all in this together." Groups also make vicarious learning possible. Participants watch, learn, and share in the work of others.

All this makes sense theoretically. If loss is the rupture of an attachment (see chapter 3), then the most powerful healing dynamic must be empathy, an emotional bonding. If loss is about a broken connection, then healing must be about reestablishing human connections. There is something very profound about the fact that the path to healing is through community, through reconnecting with others. Grief is a lonely journey, but it does not have to be. So, for all these reasons, bereaved people heal well and fast in a self-help group where they can talk with fellow sojourners. The experience of empathy communicated through genuine listening in the context of a supportive community is healing.

Telling Stories

Once bereaved people start verbalizing, something else happens. They use their words not just to vent but also to form stories. Bereaved people like to tell stories. Initially, the stories they tell are stories of how the loss occurred, especially if it was traumatic. They tell stories about the losing, all of the details of the dying and the subsequent events. Soon, the stories about *how* the loss occurred give way to stories of *what* has been lost and of their relationship with what has been lost. So, in the case of the loss of a spouse, the initial stories are of the dying and the secondary stories are of the beloved spouse. Stories are meant to be told, shared, and exchanged. Stories are shaped by the exchange of information and perspectives with family, friends, and other mourners. Stories are not static but evolve over time. They are augmented, corrected, enhanced, and embellished. Generally speaking, the stories that remain are positive stories, stories of appreciation, humor, admired qualities, and enduring traits. Some stories are still painful, but as the healing process unfolds, the stories come to reflect themes of gratitude, forgiveness, love, and even admiration.

> "The best part of the memorial service for Dad wasn't the Mass or the sermon," writes Danny, "but the reception back at Mom's. We were all relaxed then, had a few beers, and Mom pulled out the photograph albums, and we began to tell stories about Dad. Some of the stories I had heard before, a few I had never heard. Some stories made me cry, some made me laugh, and some I laughed so hard it made me cry. It was a wonderful time. We turned a sad day into a celebration of life."

The process of storying forms memories by moving the information from short-term memory to long-term memory. In grief, storying includes sorting out the truth about what has been lost, cutting through the idealization of what is lost, sorting through the degrees of responsibility for the loss, and choosing to remember the good along with the bad. The grief process closes the wounds, enabling the bereaved to remember in order to forget. Grieving can be understood as a process of bringing into consciousness memories along with their emotional overtones, verbalizing the memories, and then through verbalization integrating the memories into a larger frame of reference and releasing them back into forgetfulness. In nontraumatic losses, the memories of the bereaved are usually not so fragmented or emotionally charged as they are in traumatic losses. Yet the process is the same, although less intense. Forming stories of what is lost and telling those stories is central to the grieving and healing process. It is also a way of making meaning.

Grief stories sometimes become plays, movies, poems, or lyrics. Much of the music created in the world, particularly country music, folk music, and opera, is based on stories of lost love. Writing a song, singing a song, or just listening to a song can be a great way to facilitate one's grief work and healing. Songs uniquely blend verbalization and emotion. They touch deep emotions but also help people put words to their emotions by identifying with the story. I can easily understand why, for thousands of years, long before there were counselors, self-help books, or even clergy, songs have been the vehicles for healing. Music heals the heart, and if it is coupled with a good story, it heals all the more. Furthermore, when music is shared it reinforces the universality of grief. It gives permission to listeners and singers to access and accept their own sorrow.

Forming Memories

As stories are told and retold, they become solidified as semipermanent and then permanent memories of what has been lost, of the life that was. Venting leads to verbalization, verbalization leads to stories, and stories lead to memories. Memory making is also a way of managing pain. By placing their raw pain into stories and then solidifying those stories into memories, the bereaved create cognitive structures that hold their pain. In the process, previously charged emotions become manageable. The pain is now stored or contained. It is no longer front and center in their daily consciousness. Memories bring order to the chaos of raw emotion. At this point, it could be said that most bereaved people move from the active phase of grief to the reintegration phase. The containment of their emotions gives the bereaved more freedom to move on. For the most part, the memory formation process contains or manages grief's emotions, thus allowing people to function again.

Containers for Memories

> *The Vietnam Veterans Memorial Wall consists of two 249-foot-long polished marble walls with 58,318 names etched into the wall, the names of all the service personnel who died or are missing in action from the US conflict in Southeast Asia. The National Park Service reports that over three million people visit the memorial each year. Many come to find and trace the name(s) of a fallen comrade or loved one. When visitors search the wall to find the name of someone they knew, they also see themselves, reflected in the polished surface, searching for what was lost—the past and the present mysteriously tied together. Few pass by the wall without shedding tears. Some just sit and sob.*

A cherished memento, a photograph, a memorial, a grave site, a work of art, or a monument such as the Vietnam Veterans Memorial Wall can all function as containers for memories and thereby for the feelings associated with loss or trauma. These objects are broadly called memorabilia because they are vessels that hold memories. In that sense, they are tangible "places" that become symbolic for something intangible but powerful. In this way, they can become special, even sacred. Almost any tangible item or place can be a container for bereaved people's memories, depending on the unique history of each individual or family. By placing their pain in that physical item or place, the bereaved are able to move on. Quite literally, the bereaved can walk away from the memorial or place the cherished photograph on the bookshelf and in a sense leave their pain there. Yes, they can still revisit these places and remember again briefly, but the key is that they have now externalized their loss and can choose when they will visit it again.[9]

Special days, anniversaries, and national holidays such as Memorial Day function as grief containers too. They invite people to consolidate or limit their anguish to those assigned days so that people can function the other days of the year. When those days come around on the calendar, people can choose to enter into those feelings and memories again and then, most importantly, set them aside again the next day.

This sequence—tears, talking, empathy, storying, sharing memories, and creating containers—sounds like a linear process, but it is really much more fluid than that. Although talking leads to memory formation, remembering evokes more tears. Painful memories can be deposited or externalized into containers, but mementos can also trigger new waves of grief. The process can go in both directions: tears to memories to containers and containers to memories to tears again. Neuroscience confirms that memories, like grief itself, are actually quite fluid. Every time people remember what was lost, retell a story of what was lost, or visit a "container" place, the memories are processed again and changed ever so slightly. Yet, over time, the memories and stories associated with a painful loss become less emotionally sensitive and more ordinary. They even start to be forgotten, at first just the details around the edges, as the urgency of new life emerges. This dynamic of remembering and forgetting is part of the healing process,

---

9. The concept and term *externalize* comes from narrative therapy. For more on the value of externalization and storying as a therapeutic tool, see Madigan, *Narrative Therapy*.

too. The creation of containers for memories ultimately allows the bereaved to both remember and forget.

Complicated Grief

Over the years, various adjectives have been used to describe a healing process that has gone awry. Such terms include pathological grief, abnormal grief, contaminated grief, unresolved grief, and atypical grief. The preferred distinction these days is between normal bereavement and complicated bereavement. Complicated bereavement usually results in a prolonged grief disorder. Prolonged grief disorders are actually rare in nontraumatic bereavements.[10] They occur more often when there are preexisting psychological difficulties or when the loss event is embedded in a trauma, and the more traumatic the loss, the more likely it is that the grief will be complicated and prolonged. From my perspective, this is because people fail to successfully complete the tasks associated with trauma recovery and plunge into grief with trauma-related baggage.

A common risk factor in bereavement is depression. Mild depression or periodic mild depression is fairly common in bereavement. It is almost inevitable to feel emotionally diminished by the loss of a significant loved one. Most people work through their depressive mood in the process of healing. Others, either because of a preexisting vulnerability to depression or because the loss is central to the bereaved person's identity or self-worth, find that their grieving and healing process is sidetracked by depression. In other words, the loss has triggered a major depressive episode. Such people need professional or medical intervention to address the depression and get them back on the path of grieving and healing.

Depression and grief feel similar. They are both emotional "downers," and thus it is easy to confuse them.[11] However, dynamically they are quite different. Pure grief is focused on what has been lost. It is a longing for what is lost. It is a form of sadness that tends to dissipate over time. On the other hand, depression is more focused on the self, on a discounting,

---

10. Jordan and Litz, in their article "Prolonged Grief Disorder," report that the incidence among the bereaved of prolonged grief disorder ranges from fewer than 10 percent to 20 percent. The *DSM-5*, which prefers the construct persistent complex bereavement disorder, reports that this disorder affects 2.4 percent to 4.8 percent of the general population. American Psychiatric Association, *DSM-5*, 791.

11. The *DSM-5* distinguishes between grief and a major depressive episode along the lines I have described above. See American Psychiatric Association, *DSM-5*, 161n1.

dismissing, or negative judgment of the self. It reflects, at some level and to some degree, a chronic sense of worthlessness. Depression tends to be self-reinforcing and therefore persistent over time. It is easy to see how bereavement can trigger depression because many people assume responsibility, justifiably or unjustifiably, for the loss or death of a loved one. A mature and caring pastor can help congregants distinguish between grief and depression and can make an appropriate referral if need be.

Grief Support Ministry

Pastorally, the first responders to trauma events are often chaplains: hospital chaplains, military chaplains, disaster chaplains, police chaplains, fire chaplains, and even prison chaplains. Chaplains tend to see trauma up close and personal, and most chaplains have some training in trauma interventions and support services. Yet, a chaplain's time frame for providing services is short-term. In other words, it is a crisis-oriented ministry. On the other hand, ministers who primarily serve congregations do not tend to see trauma as often, but they do tend to see grief, lots of grief, more than they may realize. They tend to see grief up close and personal, not only the intense forms of grief but also the chronic, lingering, and unresolved forms of grief. They usually have long-term relationships with people and families in their congregations and are thus ideally situated to assist people, after most of their trauma recovery work is complete, with their equally important grief work.

There was a time in Western civilization, before the advent of modern psychology, when ministers were treated as the go-to experts on grief. Certainly, it was more of a religious age than today, and people were more likely to seek out religious solutions and guidance. I also think that people sought out pastoral services in the past because ministers knew a lot about grief, about how to comfort people and facilitate healing. After all, outside of morticians, ministers saw grief more often than any other professional group. Unfortunately, modern, younger ministers do not see themselves as experts on grief. They are quick to refer congregants to local mental health professionals and to discount the pastoral wisdom of the ages on this subject.

Ministering to the bereaved is time-consuming work. The greatest thing that a bereaved person will ask of his or her minister is time, and often that is the thing that busy modern pastors have the least of. Ministers are under pressure and are expected these days to manage the details of church programing and parish administration. It seems that there is less and less time available for providing individual pastoral care. So, I can understand why ministers often rely on lay caregivers, deacons, chaplains, and other caregivers to minister to their bereaved congregants. There is something uniquely appropriate and therapeutically powerful about believers comforting believers within the larger community of faith. Yet, at the same time, ordained clergy have an important and indispensable role to play in the context of bereavement. Whether ministers like it or not, they do represent God's love and compassion, speak for and with God, and carry the wisdom of the faith tradition.

Congregational ministers can and should do more, independently and together with their congregational caregivers, to shepherd people through their grief work. Congregational ministers are naturally and uniquely equipped with at least two resources—community and rituals—that make them ideal professionals to address the epidemic of unresolved grief in society. In chapter 2 and earlier in this chapter, I have discussed the value of community, social support, verbalization, and empathy in trauma recovery and grief work. In our modern, urbanized world, congregations are islands of community in a sea of increasing social isolation and fragmentation. As such, they can be places of support and refuge for people recovering from trauma and loss. So, anything that ministers can do to cultivate genuine community in their congregations is helpful and positive, an insurance policy for the times when congregants will need extra support. Although few congregations have the resources or expertise to offer trauma recovery programs per se and these services are probably best left to therapists or chaplains anyway, all congregations can be havens of support and healing for people in grief. Churches can and should provide grief support services and educational programing for bereaved people. Loss, death, and grief are universal and essentially spiritual subjects that lie at the heart of what it means to be fully human. A grief ministry that creates small group healing communities and occurs within the larger framework of a loving and accepting community of faith offers a rich resource for people seeking to grow in times of trauma and loss.

The second resource that ministers offer to bereaved people and families is ritualization. Rituals are as large as those held in big cathedrals and as small as individual spontaneous prayer. Rituals are both repetitive and special events. A minister's skill as a ritual artist and ritual leader can be a valuable resource for traumatized and bereaved people.

Grief Rituals

The rituals associated with death and burial have many purposes. Some ministers see these rituals as a time to preach, to teach doctrine, to reinforce beliefs, or to build loyalty to the church. Others emphasize the importance of the liturgy. Still others see death-related rituals as a time to honor the dead. And some are primarily concerned with making sure the religious practices are properly observed to ensure the eternal salvation of the deceased. Besides these worthy objectives, funeral rites are also vehicles for facilitating the healing of people wounded by the scars of trauma and loss. I therefore call them collectively grief rituals because of their therapeutic purpose.

In the sequence of death rites, the funeral or memorial service is the main event. However, many minor rituals associated with the funeral and burial process need to be considered part of the mourning process. Such rites might include choosing caskets, preparing the body, viewing the deceased, the wake, the burial, the reception, the unveiling of the headstone, and the first-year anniversary observance. All of these more minor events need to be crafted in ways that fit into the overall goal, which is to facilitate the grief work of the bereaved. In an age when there are fewer prescribed and universally accepted rituals, ministers need to give skillful attention to these minor rites, finding ways to revitalize, recreate, or craft them anew so people's needs are met. And in pluralistic or secular contexts, where there are no commonly agreed-upon rituals or burial customs or where some people do not see the value of rituals at all, ministers must be able to create and personalize rituals for grieving families. If ministers can come to see rituals, large and small, as vehicles of healing and recovery, they will be on the alert for appropriate and opportune ways to ritualize the moment. I believe that if rituals are done well, they can play a significant role in facilitating healing.

Yet, facilitating grief work through ritualization can be challenging in an age of more frequent traumas. In the audience of a memorial service for a deceased person killed in a trauma event, there may be people who themselves survived the same trauma or who also lost a family member to the same or a similar trauma; people struggling with safety issues, with moral injury, or survivor's guilt; or people who are reminded of their own victimization and traumatization in whatever form. In addition, there may be many in the gathered community who have not been particularly traumatized. They just need to grieve, need to remember, need to honor the deceased, need to revisit previous losses in their lives, and need to have ways to bring their grieving to closure. This dual focus of the funeral or memorial service—to help people feel safe and to help people grieve—is typical of the challenge of ritual events in the aftermath of a traumatic death.

Grief rituals that are helpful provide the bereaved with a safe place where they can freely express their sorrow but also feel some structure or containment for their anguish; where they are encouraged to verbalize their thoughts, questions, and doubts; where grieving families bond and support one another; where perhaps even a diverse array of people can become a community even if just for a time; where people can form, hear, and tell stories of the deceased and come to remember well; where hope and forgiveness can be proclaimed; where people's deepest anguish can be formed into words and deposited into containers and places; and where they can be connected to the cherished values, traditions, and beliefs of their faith tradition or the best of humanity. This may sound like a tall order, and it is, but it is worthy of a minister's high calling.

Finally, let me note that the aim of grief rituals might be not just to encourage grieving but also to stop grieving. In bygone eras, mourning periods with their prescribed customs placed a structure upon bereavement. People knew what to do and when to do it and *when to stop*. The sequence of customs kept people on track, preventing them from putting away their emotions too early. And the ritual at the end of the predetermined mourning period gave people permission, if not encouragement, to stop grieving and get on with their new life. Successful healing comes when people know how to grieve and how to stop grieving when the work is finished. Rituals can help with both tasks.

Reflections on Specific Rituals

Laments

Given the increased incidence of and interest in trauma, theologians have refocused ministers' attention to the ancient ritual form called lament. Laments are a form of prayer, individual or collective prayer, often used in the context of trauma, bereavement, and unjust suffering. In the Hebrew Bible, laments are found in the book of Lamentations and in the psalms of lament. Laments are complaints to God, protests of sorts, that are blended with expressions of sorrow, deliverance, and sometimes guilt. Old Testament scholar Walter Brueggemann notes that "the lamentation-complaint, perhaps Israel's most characteristic and vigorous mode of faith, introduces us to a 'spirituality of protest.'"[12] They are prayers filled with intense emotions. They are prayers of people who feel that God has let them down, that God has allowed the unrighteous to prosper while the righteous are suffering. Psychologically, prayers of lament do a good job at acknowledging and verbalizing the anger that is often embedded in grief resulting from trauma.

People who have been sinned against are drawn to prayers of lament because their traumas are the direct result of human error, human cruelty, or human sin. Andrew Sung Park, in *From Hurt to Healing: A Theology of the Wounded*, notes that Western Christianity has largely focused on those who have sinned. Weekly prayers of confession are offered for those who have sinned, coupled with assurances of pardon. Park says that the other side of the coin is those who have been sinned against, who have been victimized, who are oppressed, who have done nothing wrong themselves but are caught in the throes of loss and trauma. The psalms of lament are bold prayers, prayers for those who feel that they have been sinned against. Laments also disturb complacent Christians, shattering their denial that all is right with the world.

Spiritual Pilgrimages

"Place" is sometimes very important for those who are healing or recovering from trauma. Sometimes bereaved families or trauma survivors find it helpful to visit the place of the trauma, the site of the plane crash, the destroyed village, or ground zero. Such visits might include a return to the scene of the crime or a return to the home where they were abused as a child. Some American soldiers have recently returned to Vietnam. Others have gone to visit the concentration camp where they were imprisoned. These pilgrimages are a type of ritual. They may be done in a spiritual framework, surrounded by prayer and associated rituals.

Others, particularly in the latter phases of grief work, find it helpful to travel to a place or places unconnected to their trauma or loss. Traveling is

---

12. Brueggemann, foreword to Weems, *Psalms of Lament*, xii.

a helpful way to go on retreat from the pressures and reminders of their sorrow or tragedy. Remote places such as deserts or mountains are attractive to people seeking such solace. People who travel in this way often experience their time away as a type of "passage" from their previous pre-loss life to the new life that awaits them. It is as if they find a new place to mark their passage.

Grave sites or monuments also give people "places" on which to focus their recovery and healing. Creating a monument, whether it is done collectively or individually, helps concretize and ritualize the recovery process. It helps provide a place that trauma sufferers can visit, a place, as I said earlier, that can "contain" their raw emotions and memories. Dates are always important to people who have suffered any kind of significant loss or trauma. They seem especially important to trauma survivors. Anniversaries are important, anniversaries of the trauma itself and anniversaries of other milestones in the recovery process. Ministers who want to be supportive to people in recovery from trauma would do well to be aware of the importance of dates and places and find ways to ritualize those times and milestones.

These are challenging times for ministers in terms of pastoral care. As traumas and traumatic losses increase in frequency and intensity, the need for ritual and ritualization remains as great as ever, but modern people have fewer rituals, symbols, and customs in common. Most trauma victims or survivors do not know how to ritualize the moment. They are overwhelmed. They are emotionally vulnerable. They look to their spiritual leaders to be sensitive, caring, and wise shepherds, able to ritualize the moment in ways that bring moments of grace in the midst of healing and recovery.

Clergy Self-Care

Ministering to the bereaved is emotionally draining work. Congregational clergy, who may have two funerals and related activities in a week as well as two parishioners to visit in the hospital, feel emotionally "spent" by the end of the week... and then they have to prepare a sermon for Sunday. If ministers or lay caregivers are hospital or military chaplains who deal with these types of situations more regularly, the issue becomes even more crucial. Caring for the bereaved and traumatized is emotionally exhausting work.

Caring for the traumatized is particularly emotionally challenging. Sometimes clergy are called upon to listen to and to bear witness to horrible stories of abuse, crime, and cruelty. Deborah van Deusen Hunsinger, in her book *Bearing the Unbearable*, asks pointedly: "How do you keep your heart open when you see person after person afflicted with trauma?"[13] Those ministers who are empathetic people are especially prone to absorbing the emotions and thoughts of those they care for. How do ministers bear such burdens? Trauma gives new seriousness to the Apostle Paul's injunction to "bear one another's burdens" (Gal 6:2 NRSV).

The concept of compassion fatigue was developed some forty years ago in the context of professional nursing. It describes the gradual lessening of compassion that occurs in people in the caring professions as they become overburdened by caring for people who are suffering, who are in pain, including those who are bereaved or traumatized. In addition to lessened compassion, the symptoms of compassion fatigue include a negative attitude, hopelessness, sleep difficulties, and chronic anxiety. Statistics vary, but most caring professions report that anywhere from 12 to 40 percent of caregivers exhibit symptoms of compassion fatigue at one time or another in their career. Clergy, especially those who specialize in full-time ministries of compassion such as hospital and hospice chaplains, probably experience compassion fatigue at a similar rate.

When congregational clergy are emotionally exhausted, the term "clergy burnout" is often employed. However, burnout refers more generally to all of the demands, pressures, and stresses of ministry, whereas compassion fatigue focuses on the pastoral caregiving aspect of ministry. Compassion fatigue is often an important component of clergy burnout. Clergy burnout has become a significant problem in ministry today. It contributes to health problems among the clergy, to family and marital problems, and to the relatively high rate of ministers dropping out of ministry, and it often sets the stage for situations of clergy misconduct.

It is true that the challenges of ministry can be draining, but the significant thing to remember about compassion fatigue is that, generally speaking, the better caregivers are the most susceptible to this syndrome. That is, caregivers who are the most empathetic and most compassionate toward those who are suffering are the very persons who easily become emotionally tired. The very thing that makes ministers great at pastoral care is also the very thing that makes them vulnerable to compassion fatigue. This is what Charles Figley, who coined the term compassion fatigue, calls "the cost of caring."[14]

13. Hunsinger, *Bearing the Unbearable*, 70.
14. Figley, ed., *Compassion Fatigue*, 1.

Grief

So, what are clergy to do? How do ministers maintain their compassion and capacity for empathy when serving families in bereavement or trauma? The answer, or at least one of the answers, is self-care. Self-care includes the obvious—good health habits such as regular exercise, regular sleep patterns, limited alcohol use, and weight management. Self-care also includes being open to receiving care and support from family and friends and colleagues in ministry. More importantly still, ministers must practice their faith by practicing regular prayer and regular Scripture and devotional reading. They must practice contemplative prayer or meditation. They must take a regular Sabbath. They must find ways to genuinely worship even as they maintain their professional duties as a worship leader. This is how ministers stay open to God's compassion and God's energy.

For ministers and other spiritual caregivers, another aspect of self-care is attending to their own losses and traumas. Ministers are human beings, believe it or not! They too have lost people whom they loved dearly. Perhaps they too have been traumatized by a tragic accident, a near-death experience, an exposure to great cruelty, or even a crime. They too have their wounds. Years ago, Catholic theologian Henri Nouwen introduced the term "wounded healer" as an apt image of the work of a pastoral caregiver in the modern era.[15] Indeed, the term makes the point that sometimes people who have been wounded are better equipped to help other wounded people. That principle is generally true. It is illustrated again and again through self-help groups and programs. People who have been there are generally more compassionate toward those who suffer. At the same time, ministers need to do their own recovery work or grief work. They need to be healed of their own wounds, not necessarily completely but enough so that they are not unintentionally influencing, distorting, or even blocking the healing work of others.

Caring for the bereaved and traumatized can actually help ministers and other caregivers learn to have more compassion for themselves. In the world of grief work, the lines between caregiver and care receiver get blurry. We are all in this together. Our ability to help others grieve is related to how well we ourselves grieve. Our ability to show compassion to others is connected to our ability to show compassion toward ourselves, and both of these abilities are related to how open we are to the compassion of God. To paraphrase Scripture, the comfort we give to others in their affliction is the same comfort we receive from God in our affliction (2 Cor 1:4).

---

15. Nouwen, *The Wounded Healer*.

Questions for Personal Reflection

1. Describe your style of grieving. Are you very emotive, not very emotive, hostile, prone to depression, or plagued by guilt? How was your personal style of grieving formed in your family of origin? How did your parents or family model grief work? How does your faith tradition model grief work?

2. In your experience, what are the most helpful things to say when ministering to a newly bereaved person? What things are generally not very helpful to say?

3. Describe a ritual event that was healing to you or those you serve. How and why was it healing?

4. How honest can or should a ritual be in order to provide healing?

5. Can a funeral service facilitate grief if the body of the deceased is not present?

6. How did Jesus heal or facilitate healing among those who were suffering from emotional wounds? How did Jesus express his own sorrow?

7. Why are people embarrassed to cry in public or in church? How can ministers normalize grief?

8. List biblical passages or verses that might be used to block grief and passages of verses that might facilitate grief.

9. Read the book *Tear Soup: A Recipe for Healing after Loss* by Pat Schwiebert and Chuck DeKlyen.

10. As a caregiver, what do you do on a regular basis to refresh and renew yourself?

5

Growth

THE CHRISTIAN FAITH ASSERTS the conviction that goodness can come out of tragedy, gain can come out of loss, and growth can come out of grief. In the Hebrew Bible, we find these words from Joseph: "Even though you intended to do harm to me, God intended it for good, in order to preserve a numerous people" (Gen 50:20 NRSV). In the Christian tradition, this view is captured in the Apostle Paul's assertion, "We know that all things work together for good for those who love God" (Rom 8:28 NRSV). When a loss event is voluntary and chosen, it is easier to see the anticipated gain. This gain is why people choose the path of loss; they lose in order to gain. But when a significant loss is traumatic, it is harder to see the gain. It is harder to see how any good can come out of trauma. Even so, some people who get through their trauma recovery and grief process reasonably intact conclude that they have grown because of their ordeal. Still others can cite ways in which they are a stronger, better, and more compassionate person and have new skills and a deeper connection to God. So, how can ministers and other caregivers facilitate growth in traumatized and bereaved people?

People grow through trauma and loss in varied ways and degrees. Some do not grow at all; they simply survive the loss. Survival is good. Sometimes surviving is a kind of growing. Other people grow beyond mere survival. They learn new skills, gain new knowledge, become more resilient. A few individuals make significant changes that can only be described as transformative. Loss, even trauma, can be a catalyst for personal growth.[1]

---

1. Calhoun and Tedeschi introduced the term *posttraumatic growth* in the 1990s, and since then it has become an increasingly important area of research. See Calhoun and Tedeschi, eds., *The Handbook of Posttraumatic Growth*.

In this chapter, I am defining personal growth broadly; growth simply means that we become *better people*—not just healed people or even recovered people but better people. Growth is not just something that happens as a postlude to recovery and grief work, although that is often where it is fully realized; it is also something that occurs concurrently in and through the recovering and grieving process and in some ways can begin in the immediate aftermath of a trauma. In this chapter, I discuss some common elements or dynamics of growth. How is it that some people grow in the context of trauma and loss, whereas others do not? In the context of trauma recovery and grief work, here are three ingredients to growth. People grow when

- they reclaim their agency and empower themselves;
- they rewrite their trauma stories into survivor or growth stories; and
- they examine and reformulate their basic beliefs, values, and life assumptions.

These three dimensions of growth are applicable to the wide variety of ways people grow and to the diverse descriptions of growth. These elements tend to be interwoven processes, and for most people only one or two of the dimensions become the primary arena of their work. This chapter concludes with a brief discussion of resilience and character development.

Agency as Key to Growth

Almost by definition, trauma is something that happens *to* people, against their will; it violates their boundaries and threatens their safety. Its power can be overwhelming, rendering people powerless. Sometimes this powerlessness is relatively mild, as when first responders or therapists feel overwhelmed by witnessing the effects of trauma on others. Sometimes it is acute, as in being personally raped at knifepoint or kidnapped by enemy soldiers. Sometimes this powerlessness is temporary, lasting for a few hours or a few days, as in a natural disaster. Sometimes it is goes on for months or years, as in the case of prolonged imprisonment or torture. Regardless of these variables, trauma victimizes people. People are overwhelmed and disempowered. This lack of personal control over one's life, this robbing of one's agency, is at the heart of the experience of trauma.

Agency has been proven to be an important variable in managing change, which is, after all, what trauma and loss bring. Consider the difference between the experience of voluntary retirement vs. involuntary retirement, initiating a divorce vs. being served with divorce papers, or being an immigrant vs. being a refugee. Many losses happen to people against their will, but other losses happen because people choose it. Most losses contain a mixture of degrees of agency. Losses by choice, the losses that people choose, are generally easier to cope with and adjust to than forced losses. Or, the degree to which one can exercise choice, even within a larger context of no choice, is the degree to which one can better manage stress, process the grief, and adjust to the change. Even our own imminent death becomes more palatable if we can exercise some choice in the process. Maybe we cannot choose *not* to die, but we can choose how we will die—in other words, how we will live before we die. The experience of loss is mitigated by human agency. Even in the midst of trauma, when people are potentially overwhelmed by forces beyond their control, human agency stands as a mitigating variable. Exercising agency by making choices and taking action is easier for some people than for others, and it is easier in some trauma contexts than others. In the case of natural disasters, for example, people rally to provide aid and mobilize community resources to clean up and rebuild. Such activities, besides helping the community recover, also help people avoid becoming victimized. Action is empowering.

Impact of Prolonged Traumatization

Trauma's negative impact on human agency is more easily illustrated by prolonged traumatization, where the threat is sustained for longer periods of time. Examples of prolonged trauma are imprisonment and torture, slavery and human trafficking, a domestic relationship where the victim has been controlled over a period of time by the violence and emotional abuse of their partner, the experience of a child who is physically or sexually abused over a period of years, or even a prolonged tour of duty in a war zone. When focusing on prolonged traumas, the element of unexpectedness, which is essential to the definition of trauma, takes a back seat to the element of powerlessness. In other words, people caught in prolonged abuse or a violent situation are not very surprised by the repeated violence. Unfortunately, it becomes all too familiar. But, they cannot stop it. They cannot protect themselves. Powerlessness becomes the dominant theme.

Abusers and torturers inflict harm and cruelty to enforce their power *over* others. The victims of prolonged trauma are also rendered passive. Indeed, sometimes passivity is the best way to save one's life in the context of chronic trauma. Don't take the initiative. Don't fight back. Preserve your energy. Just survive! Sometimes victims even align with their captor, a dynamic found in the Stockholm syndrome.

Learned Helplessness

Martin Seligman first introduced the concept of learned helplessness in the 1970s to describe a condition that develops when organisms in prolonged adverse situations "give up" trying to help themselves.[2] They give up essentially because forces larger than themselves have repeatedly "beaten them down" and they have concluded, after repeated ineffective attempts at self-help or self-protection, that they have no control over the situation. Seligman suggested that such dynamics create clinical depression in animals and, more importantly, in humans. Subsequent scholars and writers have expanded upon this concept in numerous ways. Some have noted, for example, that this lack of control can be real or perceived, thus opening up for consideration the role of perception or interpretation in learned helplessness. Thus, learned helplessness can be a self-fulfilling dynamic. As might be expected, this concept has been applied to people victimized by prolonged traumas. It has been used to understand the psychological impact of prolonged victimization at the hands of a cruel and abusive spouse, parent, police officer, or prison guard or the impact on people living in oppressive economic or political environments. People learn helplessness and, in turn, learned helplessness keeps them dependent, passive, and hopeless.

People can be beaten down in a variety of ways, not always by other human beings. For the average minister or chaplain, a case in point would be someone who has to deal with a prolonged life-threatening illness and/or repeated life-threatening surgeries or medical treatments. Such people can also feel beaten down by life and may lose confidence that anything they do will make a difference, and, of course, they may become depressed. This insight and its reverse truth, the life-giving value of human agency and self-initiative, has not been lost on the health care industry. Health care professionals have come to believe that patients heal faster if they can regain control, choice, and power to the greatest extent that is possible or

2. See Seligman, *Helplessness*.

appropriate. So, hospitalized patients are increasingly encouraged to make more choices—to choose their meals, manage their own hygiene, even self-regulate their pain medicine. Sometimes little choices, little acts of self-reliance, can speed recovery. The general principle seems correct: the greater the sense of control that people have over an adverse situation, the healthier they remain and the better they are able to cope.

Chronic PTSD

Another window on the dynamics of powerlessness and the importance of agency may be found in the example of chronic PTSD. Some Vietnam veterans have been unable to recover from the trauma of war, even after some fifty years. Many have fallen into homelessness or drug addiction or suffer from various kinds of concurrent mental disorders that in turn have blocked or complicated their recovery. For them, PTSD is a chronic condition, not a temporary condition. The media have done a good job of bringing the plight of homeless vets to the attention of the public, but chronic PTSD might be more pervasive than the public imagines. Sometimes people who have been abused sexually or physically, particularly for years and particularly during their formative years, can also be understood as having chronic or recurrent PTSD. Among professionals who treat this population, the preferred term is victimization or having a "victim mentality" instead of the psychiatric label of PTSD. A victim mentality is typically characterized by low self-esteem, depression, passivity, dependency, and a sense of fatalism, and as with learned helplessness or chronic PTSD, the mentality is self-reinforcing. The more people see themselves as a victim, the less likely they are to see themselves as having any choice and the less likely they are to take any initiative to help themselves.

The psychological dynamic that keeps many people in a victim mentality is anxiety. PTSD, like all anxiety disorders, has a way of reinforcing itself. Unless people "get back on the horse" fairly soon or take some action, they can become immobilized. Their trauma-related fears become internalized, seared into the neuropathways of their brains. The good news implied in the term "learned helplessness" is that a victim mentality, fueled by chronic anxiety, is largely a learned dynamic, an adaptive response to an oppressive and dangerous environment. Most people are not inherently victims. Most people have the capacity to overcome their fears or at least manage their anxieties. The path to recovery begins with the reclaiming of personal agency.

Ministry as Empowerment

At first blush, power and empowerment might be uncomfortable concepts for most ministers. They seem to run counter to the traditional Christian virtues of humility, modesty, and obedience. But if we think about it, Jesus did a lot of empowering. He empowered the poor by being "at the table" with them over a meal. He empowered the sick by asking them to participate in their healing. He empowered the disciples by giving them a mission. He empowered the possessed by freeing them from their internal prisons. He empowered women by speaking to them and including them in his band of followers. Jesus was about empowering people, about valuing them, giving them choices, and seeing in them their gifts for ministry.

The term *empowerment* has surfaced in the literature on pastoral care and counseling in recent decades. The four traditional verbs that define pastoral care are sustaining, guiding, comforting, and healing. Some pastoral theologians, particularly from the feminist and African American perspectives, have argued that empowering is a better guiding principle for describing how clergy can be helpful when providing care to their congregants.[3] The empowerment model takes seriously social, economic, and political oppression and the impact of oppression on a person's mind-set. Trauma, especially prolonged trauma, also oppresses people psychologically. Ministers are still called to comfort and sustain those who suffer, but they also must realize that the healing of trauma includes a good dose of what biblical writers called "lifting up." Today, some of the most exciting ministries with traumatized persons are centered philosophically around the theme of empowerment.

Empowering traumatized persons can take many forms. Empowerment can be as basic as learning to walk again without assistance; it can mean taking legal action against a perpetrator; it can mean going public with your story; it can mean cleaning up debris and repairing destroyed homes; it can mean taking better care of yourself; it can mean calling yourself a survivor, not a victim; it can mean becoming an activist; it can mean helping others; and it can even take the form of getting even or taking

---

3. For example, see Wimberly and Franklin, *African American Pastoral Care and Counseling*; Neuger, *Counseling Women*; Breazeale, *Mutual Empowerment*.

revenge, although that road is filled with psychological potholes and social landmines. The action varies, but the motivation is healing. The key dynamic is agency, the reclaiming of one's power to choose and the exercising of that choice, even in adverse circumstances.

Ministers and other religious caregivers need to be sensitive to the important role that agency plays in the recovery and growth of traumatized people. Ministers can be of great assistance by giving people permission to stand up and take action and, at the same time, helping them to sort out the most mature and helpful ways to express their agency. Some ministers may unknowingly reinforce a victim mentality or learned helplessness by assuming that congregants cannot help themselves. When a congregant presents with a helpless mind-set, it is tempting for pastors to rush in and rescue him or her. "Let me find you some housing, a therapist, and a good attorney. . . . Do you need some money? Do you need Jesus? Let me help you." Rescuing a person who is already feeling helpless does not really help. It may make them dependent on their rescuer and perhaps later resist or rebel against the very assistance provided. Although it may make ministers feel good for a while, this approach may not always truly help a person in chronic PTSD or recovering from a prolonged traumatized situation. A better approach is to try to empower people. Rather than imposing solutions, strive to be a resource person. "How can I best help you?" is always a good question to ask. Another good question to ask is, "What have you learned from this experience of trauma or loss?" These questions keep the choice of and responsibility for solutions in the hands of those seeking help, even if they seemingly do not want it or do not know how to ask for help. Encouraging and celebrating people's own choices, their own sense of agency and control, helps empower them, and this renewed sense of personal power is often what traumatized persons need most.

Another common danger that many ministers need to avoid is the use or misuse of theology to reinforce victimization. A good example of this type of misuse of theology centers on the concept of the will of God. Pastors may say to the traumatized, "Well, it was the will of God" or "It was meant to be." Some misguided ministers might even tell a traumatized woman or an abused child, "It is God's will. Accept it and move on." Such pastors might mean well in that they are trying to help people accept life's misfortunes. But an emphasis on the absolute will of God undermines the responsibility of the perpetrator and the dignity of the victim. An absolutist view of the will of God tends to disempower people, to keep them oppressed.

Ministers should be careful that their implicit theological assumptions do not undermine the power and agency of victims of trauma.

For Christian caregivers, one the easiest and most direct ways to empower traumatized people is through prayer. There are all kinds of and occasions for prayer, but generally speaking prayer is healing when it honors people's experience by lifting up to God their feelings and thoughts, however raw or eloquent, positive or negative, or clear or confusing they might be. Healing prayers are not formal prayers imposed on people or the kinds of prayers that turn into sermons. Healing prayers come from the bottom up, not the top down. Prayer and all trauma-related rituals need to give victims the opportunity to "find their voice" by participating in the ritual, its creation, and its leadership. Although praying *over* people in the context of imminent threat is appropriate, in the context of healing, grieving, and growing, ministers need to pray *with* people. Praying over, even though it may represent a benevolent form of power, can be counterproductive for traumatized people.

People cannot grow when they have internalized the mind-set of a victim. Conversely, when they are empowered to make choices and do things to help themselves, however limited those choices or actions may be, people can cope with great adversity. So, the first step in facilitating growth in times of trauma and loss is to reestablish people's agency, the mind-set that they have choices, and then support them in exercising that agency. Agency empowers growth.

Survivor and Growth Stories

One of the first things that traumatized people can do to exercise agency is to tell their story. Earlier, I noted the importance of people forming and verbalizing their trauma stories. Giving voice to what one went through is empowering. It is validating, especially in contexts where the loss or trauma is producing shame and guilt. Just telling the story, especially to another human being or in a public setting, is empowering. Reclaiming and telling trauma stories is a mechanism for recovery and inevitably leads to a greater acknowledgment of what has been lost. Trauma stories are stories about *how* the loss or dying occurred. In chapter 4, I described the stories that emerge in grieving. These stories are stories about *what* was lost, stories about the life and admirable qualities of the deceased loved one or the lost entity. Over time and as agency returns, a third type of story emerges in the form of stories about the bereaved person or survivor. These are stories about the *who*, that is, the stories that people tell about themselves, their experience of recovery and healing. Survivor stories are *who* stories, stories about how the survivors have healed, grown, and/or overcome the trauma.

Survivor stories are often different from the initial trauma story. Most initial trauma stories are victim stories, stories of being victimized. As people regain agency and as they share in trauma recovery groups, they begin to reshape their trauma story in new ways. The facts remain the same, as well as they should, but the interpretation is new. Such restorying might begin early in the recovery process or not until years later, but it is a sign that the storyteller has regained a sense of agency. In truth, neuroscientists note that people are remembering and telling their story in slightly different ways all the time, but as people become empowered again, the restorying is intentional. People want to own their story.

The intentional restorying of one's trauma story might also be prompted by questions or doubts about the initial story. People may come to realize that their initial trauma story reflects some lies, such as "It's all your fault" or "I could have prevented it." Perhaps they come to understand that they have been too hard on themselves, or, perhaps, they conclude that their memory was filtered through the lens of their own personal histories and personal problems prior to the trauma. Perhaps they now see that they have understood the trauma in light of their long-standing political views or the collective ideology of their racial, ethnic, or national reference group, and they wonder whether there is another way to look at it. Maybe they have even realized that they have framed their initial story of trauma in ways that support a certain image of God, and they wonder whether they might experience God in a new way.

Care Strategies

One intervention that helps many traumatized or bereaved people is to invite them, when they are ready, to intentionally rewrite their trauma story in a way that makes them the hero or heroine of that story. Make the new story about courage in the face of suffering, about triumph over adversity. Let the facts be the same, but frame them differently. This reauthoring of one's trauma story can be done either verbally or in written form. Sometimes it takes a while, if the victim mentality is deeply embedded. This is done in private initially, but in time a telling of the revised story might be given a public audience as a ritual that celebrates healing and a new identity. Such processes can be very empowering and liberating for trauma victims.

Another intervention popular in some Christian circles is called the healing of memories, and it seeks to facilitate this same kind of restorying. Healing of memories is essentially guided imagery. It is employed with people who are caught in a resentful or depressive story of victimization, who feel they were abandoned by God in the midst of trauma. In a safe, relaxed space, under the direction of a trained professional, traumatized people are "walked through" their trauma again, but this time they "put Jesus into the scene." The facilitator might ask the following questions:

Where was Jesus in your story?

What was Jesus thinking and feeling as this trauma unfolded?

What would Jesus say to you, if he could speak then or now?

It can be difficult for Christians to know how to tell or retell their trauma story. They want to tell it truthfully, but sometimes the truth they remember is clouded by hurt, judgment, and self-incrimination.

Miroslav Volf, systematic theologian at Yale Divinity School and himself a victim of torture, suggests two principles for how Christians ought to remember their trauma stories: remember truthfully and remember rightly. Remembering rightly, at least in Volf's usage, means remembering with mercy. Volf writes, "The memory of suffering is a prerequisite for personal healing but not a means of healing itself. The means of healing is the interpretative work a person does with memory."[4] People need to be truthful about their memories and tell their trauma stories truthfully, but they also need to assign meaning or interpretation to the story that is tempered by faith in a God of mercy and compassion. In particular, Volf encourages Christians to remember the perpetrators and themselves with mercy, not judgment. Survivor stories or the restorying of trauma stories are often stories with more mercy and compassion than the initial tales of trauma. As ministers and other spiritual caregivers listen to the reshaping or reauthoring of trauma stories, they would do well to encourage a balance of truthfulness and mercy. Another dynamic associated with this retelling of a trauma story in a more merciful way is forgiveness, which I discuss more fully in the next chapter.

---

4. Volf, *The End of Memory*, 28.

Growth
Shaking of the Foundations

Humans are meaning-making creatures. We need our lives to make sense. Based on our lived experience, we make certain assumptions about life or draw conclusions to explain our lives. These assumptions can be expressed in the form of phrases or sentences that seem to capture "truths" about life. Some people formalize these assumptions into a personal philosophy or set of basic beliefs. For most people, however, these assumptions are semi-conscious; that is, they do not think about them or verbalize them until forced to or invited to by an inquisitive college professor or the life-altering challenge of trauma.

In the field of psychology, the recognition that trauma impacts a person's life assumptions received focused attention in Ronnie Janoff-Bulman's 1992 book *Shattered Assumptions: Toward a New Psychology of Trauma*. Janoff-Bulman identified three universal human assumptions that are typically "shattered" by trauma. These are: the world is benevolent, the world is meaningful, and the self is worthy. The first assumption—the world is benevolent—is built upon our primal experience of basic trust (or secure attachment), and this assumption, in whatever expression it takes, enables us to function psychologically and socially. Similarly, the second assumption—the world is meaningful—is also universally assumed. We assume that everything is explainable, that every event has a cause and effect even if it is not apparent or even if the cause and effect is in the spiritual realm. Some traumas, however, are essentially meaningless. This is the nature of trauma. Traumas are "out of the ordinary" kinds of events; events that often do not make sense, at least initially; events that shatter people's life assumptions. Generally speaking, humans hate meaning vacuums. The human need for meaning is so great, particularly in the context of great suffering, that people create their own idiosyncratic interpretations of what has happened to them. And that is not necessarily all bad. Such people are after all claiming their agency. The question is whether their trauma story remains subject to revision, new information, and new interpretations as the process of recovery and growth unfolds.

One of the significant features of Janoff-Bulman's work is her shifting the focus of trauma's impact from a person's emotions to a person's thinking. Janoff-Bulman is not alone in doing this, however. In recent decades, psychologists have continued to shine a light on the role of meaning-making in trauma recovery and bereavement. Robert Neimeyer, in his 2000 edited volume *Meaning Reconstruction and the Experience of Loss*, summarized this shift by stating that meaning-making is the "central process" in grief and trauma recovery.[5] The ability to make sense of what happened, draw lessons from what happened, and find a meaningful purpose in a post-trauma or post-loss life is critical to full recovery. I would add that the need to make sense of life is intensified in cases of trauma, in contrast to ordinary or nontraumatic bereavement. Trauma or traumatic loss, by its very definition, shatters people's ordinary life assumptions, creating, at least temporarily, a crisis of meaning.

Crises of Meaning

Because traumas or traumatic losses challenge people's life assumptions, they can trigger a crisis of meaning. The outward manifestation of that crisis is the asking of 'why' questions. Trauma has a way of triggering all kinds of "why" questions, not just about the concrete details of the trauma or loss event itself but also about the larger, more profound questions of life, what Paul Tillich called the "ultimate concerns." Humans long to make sense of a trauma on multiple levels, particularly when their experience of life does not match up with their preexisting life assumptions. Some of the deeper "why" questions that typically emerge include, why did this happen? Why now and why me? Why my loved one? Why was so-and-so so cruel? Why was I spared? Why do bad things happen to good people? Almost everyone has asked these questions at one time or another in their lives, but not everyone asks these kinds of deep "why" questions with the same degree of seriousness and intentionality. Trauma forces these questions to the surface of our minds, demanding that they be taken seriously and demanding that we respond with answers.

> Joel is an Iraq war veteran who has been through a horrible war-related trauma in which he lost most of one leg. He, along with his wife and two school-age children, are long-time church members. He struggles with chronic PTSD and particularly with finding some meaning in this tragedy. The military culture offers him several meanings, such as "You are a hero, son," "Your sacrifice will keep America free," or "Tough it out." They even pinned a medal on his chest to symbolize these meanings. He was the grand marshal in last's summer's Fourth of July parade. Yet he comes to his priest, in the privacy of the confessional, saying, "I really do not feel like a

5. Neimeyer, ed., *Meaning Reconstruction*.

Growth

hero. It was pure luck that I am alive while my buddies were blown to bits. Help me, Father, make sense of what happened in light of our faith in Christ." Joel's recovery and healing will not be complete until he finds his own answers in the context of his faith.

Most life assumptions or meanings are formed in people by their culture, their religion, and their family dynamics. The problem is not always that we have no answers to the "why" questions associated with a trauma but that the answers we have do not make sense. This is the case in the above vignette about Joel. Joel knows why he joined the military, why war is important, and why some sacrifices are necessary. Yet, in the aftermath of trauma, a life-altering trauma, Joel's previous "beliefs" seem hollow and unsatisfying. He seeks a different frame of reference for understanding his life and trauma. He wants to see what trauma looks like from a Christian perspective.

Although trauma does shake up or even shatter people's assumptive world, most people ultimately do find meaning in even meaningless traumatic events. Humans do abhor meaning vacuums. The "shattering" that Janoff-Bulman speaks of, in my experience, is usually temporary. Most people revise and/or reassert their life assumptions in the face of trauma. Others fashion new life assumptions or create new meanings in the aftermath of trauma. People can find meaning or make meaning in countless ways. For the most part, humans are remarkably resilient and inventive when it comes to meaning-making.

Religious People

Religious people, like all humans, make assumptions about life. We call them beliefs, values, or even doctrines. These assumptions or beliefs are couched in religious language and supported by biblical truths. Sometimes these assumptions correspond to formal Christian beliefs and doctrines. More often they are what Carrie Doehring calls an "embedded theology," theological assumptions that are implicit in how Christians live.[6] Like those of secular people, embedded theological assumptions can be captured in short phrases such as God is good; God will protect me from evil because I am a good person; suffering is temporary; people are essentially good [or selfish, or evil]; life is fair; life is meaningful; everything happens for a

---

6. Doehring, *The Practice of Pastoral Care*, 112. My late colleague Robert St. Clair used a similar term, "operational theology," which he contrasted with formal theology.

reason; God has a plan for my life; or God spared me for a reason. Usually, Christian truisms such as these phrases are positive and thus reassuring in times of loss and trauma, but life assumptions or embedded theology are not always phrased positively. Counterexamples are phrases such as these: if anything can go wrong it will, or, God has it in for me, or, I am a sinner.

When trauma occurs, the theological or life assumptions of Christians are challenged. Perhaps a believer had always assumed that life is fair, but a particular traumatic event was so unfair, so unjust, that he or she now questions that belief. Or, perhaps a believer had always assumed that God would protect him or her, but a particular traumatic event was so horrific, so random, that they now question their embedded trust in God's providence. In the aftermath of a trauma, some Christians examine their embedded theological assumptions and determine that their theology held up fairly well in the midst of the trauma. Perhaps they had thought about these possibilities before. They had some reasonable answers to the "why" questions, answers that helped them make sense of what happened and guided their recovery. Other Christians, maybe Christians who are facing trauma for the first time in their lives or are young in their faith, may feel shaken or even shattered by the trauma experience. If their faith is shattered, they may drift away from religion. Or perhaps they openly struggle with these theological issues, examining and reexamining the tenets of their faith and flushing out their embedded assumptions into the light of day. For them, this quest to find meaning will be central to their recovery and healing processes. Either way, though, whether believers reaffirm their pretrauma theological assumptions or refashion a new set of theological assumptions, they all emerge from trauma recovery with more of what Carrie Doehring calls "deliberative theology," a set of life assumptions or beliefs that are consciously thought out, chosen, and embraced. Trauma demands that every believer reexamine or revisit life's most basic theological assumptions. Ministers and other Christian caregivers can be helpful when they acknowledge that struggle and offer to walk alongside the believer and search together for answers that make sense and that will help the believer grow in his or her faith.

Building Resilience

The entire process described in this book—trauma recovery, loss acknowledgment, grief work, and even the growth work described in this chapter—is hard work. Not everyone completes this process in its entirety. Many more complete it partially. When people do complete or mostly complete this process, we say that they are building resilience. They become stronger so that the next time a trauma or loss impacts them, they can respond better.

There is much interest these days in resilience. Popular bookshelves are lined with books on resilience. The military, for example, would like to be able to identify recruits who will be resilient in the face of trauma on the battlefield so that there will be a lower incidence of or damage from PTSD. Some people think that resilience is a trait people either have or do not have, that some are born with a gene for resilience. I believe that resilience is not something we are born with but something we develop. For most people, resilience is something they learned in the course of their formative and early adult years, but it is never too late to build resilience. Adults can build resilience by faithfully completing the recovery, grief, and growth work described in this book again and again, and each time they become a little stronger, more resilient, and more capable. They acquire resilience-based skills.

Another word for resilience might be *character*. When I survey the literature on resilience, I note that there are many skills or personality traits associated with resilience. These skills include a hopeful, positive attitude; a sense of personal agency; reaching out for social support; accepting yourself (not blaming yourself); releasing resentments; self-soothing (managing anxiety); good health habits; avoiding substance abuse or overuse; a sturdy belief system that makes sense of tragedies; and creative, adaptive thinking. Many of these trauma-resistant traits sound a lot like traditional Christian virtues. In *The Road to Character, New York Times* columnist David Brooks reminds us that character is born or developed through encounters with suffering, hardship, and even traumas. Trauma tests us and gives us the opportunity to build character and resilience. Modern Western culture does not focus much on character development in adults or children. The emphasis is more on making us good consumers than it is on making us sturdy souls. No wonder modern people seem to be so susceptible to the negative impact of traumas. Perhaps this is the mission of the church in the twenty-first century—to focus anew on character development, cultivating in people the virtues and the skills to not only cope with trauma but to transcend it.

Questions for Personal Reflection

1. How have your experiences of trauma, loss, and grief made you a better person?
2. What biblical characters or passages might you use to empower someone or help them reclaim their agency?
3. Reflect on an experience in which you felt mistreated, abused, or hurt. You probably know this story well, but take the time to write out the story in a new way and make yourself the hero or heroine of the story. Without changing the facts, interpret them in a way that highlights your character and resilience.
4. What are your top five fundamental assumptions or basic operational beliefs (not the formal beliefs you affirm in worship but the beliefs you actually live by)?
5. Make a list of written resources that might be helpful to someone struggling with difficult questions of meaning in the context of trauma or unmerited suffering.
6. What Scripture passages or biblical characters are good role models for making sense of a senseless trauma?
7. Which is more important: to remember truthfully or to remember mercifully?
8. Which character traits or skill sets have helped you cope with trauma and significant losses in your life?
9. Do some research on the distinction between embedded theology and deliberative theology. Identify an example or two from your life or ministry that this distinction helps to clarify.
10. Do you agree with the assertion that humans can endure almost any "what" if they have a "why"? Is this true of your life and experience with trauma?

6

Spirituality

AT FIRST GLANCE, ONE might think that trauma and spirituality are not compatible dynamics, but as I have already said several times, trauma has a way bringing people to their knees. Trauma and significant losses have a way of shaking up the foundations of people's lives, initiating a process that either results in a deeper, richer, and more vibrant faith or the gradual loss of faith in the sea of despair and cynicism. It is interesting to note that the advent of trauma studies in the last thirty years has been paralleled by a reemerging interest in spirituality in the United States. Evidence of this interest in spirituality is reflected in the increased popularity of Buddhist-based practices such as mindfulness meditation (which has been proven to be helpful in trauma recovery), a renewed interest in spiritual direction among Protestant and Catholic Christians, and the continuing growth of Spirit-based worship in Pentecostal and non-Pentecostal churches. All this is occurring as the incidence of trauma rises all around us.

For purposes of this chapter, I am defining spirituality as an individual's relationship with God and God as that which is transcendent, holy, and beyond oneself. Spirituality is not theology, although spirituality has a cognitive component. Spirituality is more about the experience of the divine in one's life. In this chapter, I explore three pathways for spiritual growth that can occur in the process of trauma recovery and grief work. These three pathways are (1) discovering a benevolent God, (2) forgiveness work, and (3) embracing gratitude. These pathways have something in common: they all describe various ways that God draws close to the wounded heart, to paraphrase Psalm 34.

The process of trauma recovery and grief work is not complete without some soul work, some attention to the ways that the experience of trauma and loss has damaged or changed a person's spirituality or has invited them to a new kind of spiritual life. Ministers and other spiritual caregivers can be especially helpful in bringing a spiritual dimension to recovery and grief work. At the same time, most caregivers agree that few people do much soul work in the context of trauma recovery and grief work. Most people do what they have to do to function again and deny, avoid, or delay working on the other issues. For those who are open to some soul work, either during the process of trauma recovery or later, the following sections suggest three roads that ministers can invite them to travel in their search for a deeper spiritual life, three roads that will open them up to a deeper relationship with a compassionate God.

Discovering a Benevolent God

Most humans assume that life is predictable and good. Erik Erikson calls this assumption basic trust. He suggests that basic trust is initially formed in the first few years of life, and, as such, it is preverbal and precognitive. It was not something we thought out or thought about when we were infants; it was something we experienced. Erikson suggests that the primal "conflict" between basic trust and basic distrust is never completely resolved, and we revisit it at every stage of life. In other words, there are always elements of mistrust in everyone's soul. Religion, among other things, is an institution that sustains and renews people's basic trust. Believers call this basic trust "faith." Faith is trust in God, in God's goodness and predictability. It is our assertion that God is good and faithful.

Most healthy, stable believers have a faith history, a history of experiences in which God has been faithful, steady, and merciful. Most believers have a storehouse of trust and faith to draw upon to get them through times of mistrust. And for those with eyes to see, trauma may actually strengthen their faith by adding to their trust history because they can point to ways that God has been merciful even in the midst of trauma, loss, and sorrow. For many others, experiences like trauma, loss, and sorrow shatter their trust in God's goodness, at least for a time, and sometimes for a lifetime.

Most Christians are raised to have an absolutist view of God. This is the orthodox and most popular understanding of God among Christians.

Spirituality

It is also reinforced because our earliest experiences of trust, good or bad, are with our parents. Even though we later come to see our parents' limits and faults, our earliest experience of them is that they are all-powerful, all-knowing, and, hopefully, all-loving people. Similarly, Christians believe that God is all-powerful, all-loving, and completely in charge, as our parents were in the first few years of our lives. Many Scripture references and Christian writers support this understanding of God. As a result, when most Christians encounter trauma, they assume God will protect them or at least knows what's going on. More precisely, they treat this assumption as a kind of unspoken compact, "If I trust God, God will provide and protect me. That's the deal!" Like Job, most Christians have faith in an absolutist God and thus wonder why God did not protect or provide for them or, in some cases, even show up. From these questions, they can draw several false conclusions.

God Is Not Trustable

One conclusion could be that God is not trustable because God either brought on or at least allowed the trauma or traumatic loss. Even when the suffering is caused primarily by a human being, Christians can still believe that God allowed it. God could have stopped it. God failed to keep the compact to protect and provide. This conclusion alone drives many Christians out of the organized church, saying, "I can no longer believe in a God who would allow such suffering" or "God was nowhere to be found in the midst of my horror" or "God was silent, powerless, a toothless tiger in the face of evil." This is a challenging theological conundrum and is central to the task of healing and growth for traumatized Christians. It is a problem in part because people have an absolutist view of God and in part because they have a history of experiences of broken trust that block them from being able to experience trust.

Trauma Is Evil

Almost by definition, trauma is an experience of an overwhelming power that causes death and destruction. So, it is relatively easy for some Christians to conclude that "trauma is evil." In some ways, evil is an appropriate adjective for many of the horrors perpetrated by other human beings, such as abuse, torture, and unbelievable cruelty. I sympathize completely with the victims of such crimes, who feel as a victim once said to me, "I was staring at evil... there was no other explanation for it." Feeling that trauma is evil is more of a gut response than an intellectual response. Nevertheless, I offer three observations. First, employing the term *evil* is making something complex quite simple. Most traumas have multiple causes on multiple levels. Evil is a simple, albeit convenient, answer to a complex subject. Second, employing evil as an explanation for trauma is appealing because it lets God off the hook. Trauma does not come from God; it is the doing of the Evil One. God is thus allowed to be completely on the side of the victims, standing fast against evil. Third, when evil is used as an adjective to describe a person or group of persons, not just an event, new problems arise. Attributing trauma to evil people is dangerous. It implies that some people are good but others are evil. Such dualism sets the stage for and justifies revenge. If "they" are evil, then any revenge believers might inflict upon them or their families is justified. That kind of thinking has fueled many a genocide. I think that it is best to employ the term *evil* to describe events, a situation, larger societal forces, and even behaviors, but not particular people.

God Is Punishing Me

When trauma happens, many Christians conclude or at least wonder whether it is their fault. This is a common response to adversity that is otherwise unexplainable. It is also a common response among children, who naturally have an absolutist view of their parents. "I must have done something wrong," or, at the least, "I must have been in the wrong place at the wrong time." "I should have known better." The religious corollary to "It's my fault" is "God is punishing me." "God is punishing me [or us]" is a response with a long history in the annals of human religion. For eons, this idea prompted believers to double down on their religious practices by making more or better sacrifices, increasing ritual observations, and complying more strictly with moral and legal rules... all in the hope of drawing favor with the gods. This is an explanation that is often found in Scripture, too. It is still a common response among Christians from legalistic and moralistic traditions or people with a predisposition for self-incrimination or children under the age of twelve. It is not always a logical response to trauma, but then again, trauma is by definition so unexplainable, so meaningless, that this conclusion seems to be the only logical explanation.

One of the pioneering researchers in the psychology of religion is Kenneth Pargament, emeritus professor of psychology at Bowling Green State University. He has spent his entire career applying empirical, scientific methods to the study of how religious people cope with the stress triggered by crisis or trauma. Based on his research, he has identified three styles of religious coping.[1] His three styles of religious coping reflect three assumptions about the will of God:

1. defer to God: Nothing happens in life that is not God's will. God's power is strong. Furthermore, God's will is always good.
2. self-directed: God is helpless or weak in the world, for whatever reason. Therefore, people need to solve their own problems.
3. collaborative: God and humans are co-creators; they share power and are limited by each other's power to shape events and take actions.

Pargament has documented that believers with an absolutist view of God do not cope as well as people with a more collaborative view. People with an absolutist understanding of God might, in the face of trauma, conclude, "Well, it was the will of God" or "It was meant to be" or, even worse, "God must be punishing me." Some believers might conclude that their suffering is a deserved punishment; others jump to this conclusion because there is no other explanation for their trauma. Either way, people who view God as vengeful or punishing do not cope as well in times of stress and crisis as people with *a more benevolent view of God*.[2] Having a more benevolent view of God is linked to having a less absolutist view of God, meaning that not everything that happens is considered God's will.

Strategies for Spiritual Care

A generation ago, when the study of grief was in its infancy and the study of trauma had not even begun, professionals understood "why" questions as manifestations of anger, a component of grief. When a bereaved or traumatized person lashed out, asking, "Why has God done this to my family?,"

---

1. Pargament, *Psychology of Religion and Coping*, 293.
2. Pargament, *Psychology of Religion and Coping*, 226–29.

clergy were advised to respond to the emotion, not the content, saying, "You are really angry. I understand that you are frustrated and want some answers." Clergy were advised not to provide answers or even address the question theologically. In more recent decades, as noted in earlier chapters, even secular scholars have come to understand that mourning does have an important cognitive or meaning dimension. Of course, there are still times, particularly in the midst of acute grief, when the "why" questions still need to be understood as emotional venting, not as genuine questions. But sometimes these questions are genuine and sincere, and answering them does help people find meaning in a meaningless event. Such work is an important part of the recovery and healing process.

Furthermore, answering theological questions or at least giving theological guidance is one of the tasks that ministers understand to be central to their pastoral work. Ministers are trained to give answers to some of life's most baffling moral and theological dilemmas. In many denominations or cultural contexts, this is also a social expectation of the role. Rather than give pat answers, even tried and true answers, I find it to be more helpful to support people in their search to find satisfying answers. First and foremost, ministers must listen in order to help people clarify the issues and offer resources for their search. They can then point congregants to Scripture passages or biblical characters who faced similar situations. They can provide books, sermons, or written materials in which theologians, poets, and mystics wrestle with these issues. They can even suggest novels or movies that raise these questions. They can encourage them to dialogue with other people of faith within the congregation or with others who have experienced the same or a similar trauma experience. Most of all, ministers can encourage people to offer these questions up to God in prayer with openness, humility, and a genuine attitude of seeking. It is important that ministers be open to and supportive of each person's unique journey of faith.

I do think that finding theological answers is an important part of trauma recovery and grief work. But I have found that sometimes rigid or overly intellectual stances, however theologically sound, can be a barrier to healing as much as a balm. Believers who have come through horrific trauma and loss experiences with a deeper faith often have done so not because they have *thought about* God differently but because they have *experienced* God differently. They have experienced a compassionate, loving, and merciful God who is not up in the heavens but is present in their suffering.

Spirituality

> *Mr. Johnson is dying. When nurses or doctors enter his hospital room, he is noticeably irritable and grouchy. He complains a lot about everything and nothing. His father always taught him to be the master of his own fate—"Control your destiny"—but now he can't control anything, not even his bladder. When his immediate family visits, he says very little. He is stoic and sullen out of a misplaced desire to spare them the anguish of the situation. The chaplain reminds him that he mustn't give up hope. "The doctors are bound to come up with something." Mr. Johnson's response is usually a cynical remark. No one can possibly know what it is like to be out of control, to be finite, to feel robbed by life. One of the more helpful questions that the chaplain poses to Mr. Johnson is, "Where has God showed up in the last few years of your sickness?" Mr. Johnson predictably responds, "Nowhere . . . how could God be with me, given what has happened?" The chaplain keeps returning to the theme, finally encouraging Mr. Johnson to mull on the question a bit, look again at his life, and consider alternative story lines or information. After reflection, Mr. Johnson tentatively shares a story of a kind word, an unexpected friend, an answered prayer, and a sound night of sleep wherein he experienced the presence of God.*

The question posed in the above vignette—"Where has God shown up?"—invites people to focus not on theology but on spirituality. Ultimately, I think that most people resolve these questions around theodicy not with a rational argument but through a change in their experience of God, i.e., through their spirituality, not their theology. What typically happens is that in the process of bereavement or trauma recovery, people experience God differently, or a different side of God or perhaps even a different God, and this experience informs and shapes their beliefs about God.

> *Elena Reyes lost her youngest child, her seventeen-year-old son, in a fire at a nightclub where he had gone with his friends to dance. Even though the funeral Mass was a splendid, heart-wrenching affair, Elena continued to suffer. She regularly had nightmares of Luis screaming as the fires surrounded his trapped body. Often the dream ended with her inability to get to him, to protect him, to save him. She declined a sleep aid that her physician prescribed, saying, "It is not our way." Over the weeks and months, she lost weight, became tired and pale, stopped working at the family business, and withdrew from her family. She had attended Mass very regularly until her son died. Her priest reported that he did see her weekly on Wednesdays, when she would come to church, light a candle for Luis,*

and sit quietly in the pew. Sometimes he would try to engage her in a conversation, and if she shared some of her "bad dreams," he tried to reassure her that her son's death was not her fault. On one occasion, she said that she thought God was punishing her for some unspoken offense. The priest invited her to come to confession the next day, but she did not show up.

Weeks and months passed. The situation seemed stable, so the priest was surprised when Elena called the parish office and asked for an appointment. "Padre," she said in a trembling voice, "she came to me . . . our Lady of Guadalupe, the mother of all sorrows." Jesus' mother, Mary. "She came to my bedroom, standing there as bright as the day, with tears in her eyes. . . . She knows . . . she knows what it is like to lose a son."

This was the turning point in Elena's recovery and healing. From that day forward, she began to open up more, re-engage with her family, and attend Mass on Sundays. The priest considers her vision a small miracle.

Trauma, traumatic loss, or any significant loss experience can shape how people experience God, as the above vignette illustrates. Elena's anxiety, pain, and suffering related to the traumatic death of her son blocked her from experiencing the love and presence of God, even though she had had a fairly positive relationship with God prior to the tragedy. Elena has many questions about God's role in her tragedy, but mostly she is just confused, like most traumatized people, disconnected from God on an emotional and spiritual level. Her vision of Mary, Mother of Jesus, empathizing with her loss, was a gift. This was God showing up in an unexpected, mystical way. Her vision helped her experience a compassionate God, or, to put it differently, the compassionate side of God.

Generally speaking, I find that, for people of faith, their experience of God changes in a more compassionate direction in the course of recovery from trauma or loss (see figure 5). If anything, people who have passed through a trauma or a traumatic loss have fewer and less certain answers to the "why" questions, but often they do have a stronger experience of God. As a trauma survivor once said to me, "I have fewer answers now. I have become an agnostic when it comes to the great questions of life, but I have an experience of God's presence, and without that presence, I would not be here today."

Spirituality

Figure 5
Faith: Before and After Trauma

BEFORE		AFTER
Absolutist God	→	Benevolent God
God as Caesar	→	God as Fellow Sufferer
Transcendent God	→	Immanent God
Focus on the Will of God	→	Focus on the Presence of God
Masculine Side of God	→	Feminine Side of God

I am not saying that one view of God is more correct than another. I am only saying that most people who come through trauma with a deepened and more vibrant faith do so because they experience another side of God, a more compassionate, present, and personal God. For some, this shift will be dramatic; for others, it will be more gradual.

There is a *Peanuts* cartoon in which crabby Lucy is looking toward the heavens, raising her fist in anger at God, complaining about something. All the while, Snoopy is passionately hugging her leg. She is so focused on the heavens, on her all-consuming anger at God, that she fails to see the presence of God in the faithful love of Snoopy. In times of trauma and loss, people look for God in all the wrong places. They see only the all-powerful, absolutist God and fail to see the compassionate, benevolent God who comes to them in moments of grace and human support. The calling of ministers and other spiritual caregivers is not just to be good listeners, or even to be Snoopy, but to help people have the eyes to see God's compassionate presence in the midst of trauma and loss.

Forgiveness Work

Traumatized people or people in the midst of traumatic bereavement often feel quite angry, especially if they perceive the trauma event or loss to be unjust, unusually cruel, or even just unexpected. People feel violated by trauma. By nature, trauma is aggressive. It does not knock on the door waiting for permission to enter; it smashes down the door! Understandably, people can feel violated.

The degree of anger that people experience depends on the nature of the trauma or loss and the person's predisposition to hostility. Anger can take many forms. Sometimes it is overt; sometimes it goes inward, contributing to depression or somatic illnesses. Anger can be explosive, or it can take the form of chronic, low-grade resentment. Sometimes it has specific targets; sometimes it is free-floating hostility. Generally, anger seeks a target. People want to be angry *at* something, *at* someone. In many trauma and traumatic loss situations, it is difficult to know who or what to be angry with . . . the deceased, ourselves, or God. One of the motives in getting the trauma story straight, which I talked about in chapter 2, is clarifying who is responsible, i.e., who to be angry at. Sometimes, it is very clear: the target of the anger is the shooter who took the child's life, the drunk driver, the pilot of the airplane, the abuser, or the politicians. Sometimes, the fault is shared among those who should have stopped the perpetrator, should have prevented the tragedy, should have arrived faster, or should have warned people. In the context of trauma, people tend to want to find someone to blame.

Anger is not always a bad thing. Sometimes anger is appropriate, motivating, and empowering. But anger in the context of trauma easily fuels revenge. When people have been hurt, they want to hurt back. They want to strike at those whom they blame for their suffering or their loss or for threatening them. If particular individuals are not identifiable, then traumatized people may target particular racial groups, nationalities, or religions. "They are the ones who did this!" The world is filled with examples of individuals and groups of people exacting revenge upon groups of people whom they perceive to be responsible for a trauma.

Revenge can be very motivating—just ask any coach or military commander. It is interesting to note that the pleasure areas of the brain light up when people think about getting even. Revenge can give people a sense of closure to their grief process. If we exact revenge either on the battlefield or in the courts, then "justice has been served" and the wounded can get on with their lives.

If only that were the case! If the revenge is actually an eye for an eye, then a more apt term than *revenge* might be *justice*. If the winning is revenge for a loss, then the winning players have "gotten even." It seems fair. The trouble with trauma, however, is that trauma by its very definition is an event that is out of the ordinary realm of human experience. Trauma is too much horror, too much cruelty, too much gruesomeness, too much death and suffering. So the vengeful response to trauma is often overkill. People do not take a life for a life; they take out a whole village. People do not inflict suffering in proportion to their suffering; they inflict a greater amount of suffering. People want to see the offending party really suffer, not just receive justice. The emotions surrounding trauma are intense, so revenge in the context of trauma is often overkill.

Revenge is also intensified or made more likely by social or cultural dynamics. In short, revenge is a tribal thing. Group pressures and expectations turn what would have been a normal anger response to trauma into revenge. When individuals come to believe that their personal trauma is part of a larger attack upon their ethnic, racial, or religious group, the dynamics of revenge are intensified and sustained. That interpretation of reality is sustained by collective victim stories, which almost always require a vengeful response.

The modern civilized world tries to channel a victim's desire for revenge into the legal system, whether the victim is an individual or a group of people. Civilized nations strive to grant justice, not revenge; they aim to limit revenge to "an eye for an eye." Yet there is a thin line psychologically between justice and revenge. To my mind, revenge is a broader concept than just behavior, as bad as such behavior can be. Revenge also includes a vengeful attitude, chronic hatred, or bitterness. The criminal justice system may grant a victim some measure of justice and prohibit retaliatory violence, but the problem of revenge is also psychological and spiritual. Even in the world of religion, revenge is more widespread than the obvious acts of revenge we see reported on the news. Many people live with a chronic vengeful attitude, a chronic resentment or bitterness that pervades their emotional life for years and years.

What Is Forgiveness?

Forgiveness is central to the Christian message and the Christian path to healing. Forgiveness is understood in various ways. Many Christians, as did the Apostle Paul, understand forgiveness in a legal framework. Forgiveness is pardon. Forgiveness is letting someone off the hook legally or morally. Forgiveness is waiving their deserved punishment. Many other Christians understand forgiveness in a relational framework. In this framework, forgiveness is to be preceded by confession and an apology from the offending party. Forgiveness then is a response and the next step toward reconciliation. Jesus often approached forgiveness with this framework in mind (see

Matt 18:21–35; Luke 15:11–24). Some victims of prolonged trauma have a hard time with this notion that forgiveness must lead to reconciliation.

Still other Christians approach forgiveness from a psychological or spiritual framework. Forgiveness is about the cleansing of one's heart and mind. Forgiveness has more to do with the forgiver than the offender. People forgive for their own sake, to heal themselves of anger and resentment. The word *forgive* means literally "to give back." What are trauma survivors giving back? Definitely, they are giving back their resentment and their right to revenge. In forgiving, they are letting go of their right to take and/or nurture a vengeful attitude. They are replacing revenge with shalom. Forgiveness does not mean that trauma victims have to completely forget what happened. It means that they remember it in a new way, without bitterness or resentment.

Forgiveness and Grief Work

Forgiveness is difficult. It cannot even begin until people recognize and acknowledge their hurt. Clearly, a vengeful attitude or even vengeful behavior can be a way of avoiding or denying the pain associated with loss and trauma. It can be a way of avoiding doing grief work. It can be a way of keeping the focus out there on those others who are "the problem" instead of focusing on what is happening emotionally inside of oneself. This use of revenge, as a defense mechanism against the pain of loss, is typically more of a male dynamic than a female one. In Western culture, men generally have a harder time allowing themselves to be vulnerable and weak and seek to hide their vulnerabilities in threats tinged with false bravado or violence. Women are socialized to be more comfortable acknowledging and expressing their woundedness and are thus more open to grief work and less likely to pursue vengeful behavior. Yet, if revenge is more than behavior but also an attitude, both genders are equally susceptible to the perils of revenge.

Grief work, then, is a prerequisite for forgiveness work, or it should at least occur concurrently. If bereaved or traumatized people want to get well, to find inner peace, they must shift their focus away from identifying who is to blame and onto themselves, onto their own hurt. When they make that shift, they begin to cry and they begin to heal. Forgiveness is difficult because it takes some time. It cannot be rushed or embraced within the first few days of a trauma or one's release from a prolonged trauma. It is made possible by recovery work and grief work and, like recovery work

Spirituality

and grief work, it is more of a process than an event. Most people need some time to feel safe again, to trust again, to be clear about their trauma story, and to process their hurt and their angry feelings. Then, in time, they come to a point where forgiveness is an option. It is more likely to occur toward the latter stages of healing than in the immediate aftermath of a trauma. Another reason why forgiveness is more likely to occur in the latter phases of healing is that forgiveness is a type of forgetting, of forgetting the offenses and the horror of what happened. Earlier, I noted that traumatized people first need to remember fully, and to remember well, and only then are they able to truly forget. "Forgive and forget" is possible, but only after one has fully remembered the horrors and cried over the losses.

> *Pastor Jackson is a lay minister, associated with the Prison Fellowship program, who leads a restorative circle at the state prison. In this circle, six people who have lost loved ones by murder and two community leaders meet for conversation with six and sometimes as many as ten inmates serving time for murder. This week, Jasmine tells her story of how her husband's murder in an aborted robbery of their family has impacted her life. She tells of the family's bankruptcy, her employees who lost their jobs, her depression, one of her teenager's difficulties with the law. The inmates listen attentively. After she finishes, two inmates share something of their lives, their regret over their crimes. Later, one of them (although he was not the offender in Jasmine's case), apologizes to her, saying, "I had no idea how much damage one stupid decision can cause people." Jasmine replies, "I too had no idea how much some of you guys have been through." The group agrees to meet again next week and continue the conversation for the remaining four prescribed sessions.*

I am not sure that trauma victims like Jasmine can participate in programs such as restorative justice without first doing some of their personal recovery and grief work. Forgiveness work cannot be rushed or embraced as a way of avoiding one's legitimate angry feelings. Some trauma survivors stay stuck in low-grade depression and resentment for years and years precisely because they have never been willing or invited to enter into the forgiveness process. Forgiveness must be chosen, an intentionality of the heart and soul. My sense is that, for people like Jasmine, forgiveness work is the logical next step in their healing process.

Regardless of whether or how one engages in forgiveness work, it is not easy. Forgiveness is not natural for most people ("To err is human, to forgive is divine"). Forgiveness work includes regular prayer, Scripture reading, and meditative work. Some people, however, may never forgive. They choose not to forgive or decide not to forgive. It may be all they can do simply to "not repay anyone evil for evil" (Rom 12:17 NRSV).

The above vignette also reminds us that forgiveness should not be understood as resignation or an act of submission to oppression, nor should it be done in an apologetic manner. Forgiveness can and should be empowering. Forgiveness is an act of choice, an intentional choice by a free person to stand up and move on. It must always be voluntary. Forgiveness is a way of affirming one's self, a way of choosing the direction of one's life from here on. It is a way of saying, "Okay, this trauma happened, but I choose to not let the trauma control my well-being any longer. I choose to put away the resentment, hurt, and victimization." Forgiveness should be empowering.

Forgiving Yourself

After a series of sermons on forgiveness for the Lenten season, Heather approaches her minister saying that these sermons were disrupting her sleep. She asks, "Is forgiveness always necessary or even possible?" She relates the story of how she was sexually molested as a young teen by her paternal grandfather, who began living with the family right after her parents divorced. The molestation occurred occasionally, a few times a month, usually at night, during the years when she was thirteen to sixteen years old. It mostly involved serving the grandfather's needs. When Heather objected, her grandfather threatened to tell her mother how promiscuous she was. Heather felt frightened, repulsed, and shamed. She had trouble sleeping then, too. In time, when she was sixteen years old and after hearing about child abuse in school, Heather did tell her mother. Her mother immediately kicked her father-in-law out of the house but did not formally report the abuse to anyone. Heather's mother really did not want to talk about it, and so they did not. Nor did Heather get any professional treatment. Everyone just moved on, and maybe that is one reason why Heather was so relieved to go away to college. Heather did talk about it with friends over the years, and certainly with her husband when she married. All seemed fine until she got a phone message a few weeks ago that her grandfather was ailing and perhaps near death. She dismissed this message as something she did not want to respond to. She just ignored it . . . or so she thought. But as she listened to the sermons on forgiveness, she wonders whether

Spirituality

Christ wants her to reconcile with her grandfather. Is it is her Christian obligation to forgive?

By virtue of the nature of their trauma or by their own predisposition, some people cannot, will not, and probably should not forgive (pardon) the people responsible for their victimization. That may be the case with Heather, in the above vignette. A deeper conversation with Heather is in order. At the very least, Heather needs to be reminded that forgiveness is not the same as reconciliation. Forgiveness is not something Heather does for her grandfather but something she does for herself. In their popular manual on how to heal from the trauma of childhood abuse, *The Courage to Heal: A Guide for Women Survivors of Child Sexual Abuse*, Ellen Bass and Laura Davis write, "It is *not* necessary to forgive the abuser in order to heal from child sexual abuse. The only person you have to forgive is *yourself*."[3] Maybe, as Bass and Davis suggest, Heather's primary focus should not be on forgiving the offender but on forgiving herself.

Guilt and shame are two other emotions that are often present in grief and trauma recovery work. Inevitably, traumatized or bereaved people ask questions such as, Did I do something wrong? Did I fail to take precautions? Could I have stopped this tragedy? Did I not follow directions? Did I act badly, like a coward, or allow fear to overcome me? Was I being punished? Was I not strong enough? Often, these questions get answered in the process of forming, telling, and receiving trauma stories or stories about the dying. A good trauma story identifies the relative degree of responsibility for the tragedy. The answers are not always clean. In all honesty, some bereaved or traumatized people do conclude that they were partially to blame, either by a sin of commission or omission. They must learn to forgive themselves. Still others conclude that they are to blame, but most reasonable people would say otherwise. They too need to learn to live with their internal critic. Whatever the circumstances, it seems to be that trauma and traumatic loss seem to intensify guilt and shame, as they do so many of the emotions associated with grief.

---

3. Bass and Davis, *Courage to Heal*, 171, emphasis in the original. The quotation implies an understanding of forgiveness more as pardon and release of oneself than as the forgiveness of another that I have presented here.

Survivor's Guilt

Sometimes trauma survivors experience what is commonly called survivor's guilt. They feel guilty that they lived while others perished. Their house was spared in a raging fire while their neighbors' homes burned to the ground. They walked away from the plane crash, but dozens died. They came home, but their buddies died in a foreign land. Survivor's guilt is a mixture of guilt, gratitude, and relief, all mixed into one ambiguous emotion. Survivor's guilt may be compounded by the assumption that the survivor does not deserve to live. "Life is supposed to be fair, and I am not a better person than my friend who died." Survivor's guilt begs the question, Why was I spared? Such questions strike at the heart of one's assumptions and core beliefs. Many people resolve this guilt by concluding that they were spared for a greater purpose or, as one colleague said, "God still has a purpose for my life." Sadly, a few are not able to forgive themselves and muddle on thinking, either consciously or unconsciously, that they should have died in place of the deceased.

Moral Injury

In recent years, the term *moral injury* has entered the discussion of trauma recovery. This concept has emerged in the context of the battlefield, where soldiers may be ordered to kill other human beings in a way or to such a degree that the soldiers feel that they have violated their own sense of right and wrong. Certainly, killing in a war theater is justified; after all, it is war, it is "kill or be killed," it is advancing a greater good. Nevertheless, some soldiers feel that their personal morality has been compromised. They feel a deep sense of guilt and shame over what they did and/or failed to do. Indeed, there is something deeply shameful about doing what soldiers sometimes have to do. This may explain why many soldiers, from all wars, are often reluctant to talk much about their war experience.

National Public Radio recently described moral injury as the "signature wound" of our times, stating that it occurs because war is being waged in an age of terror, an age when the principles of the Geneva Convention are being ignored by many combatants. Modern soldiers who witness the random murdering of innocent civilians, rape of women, abuse of children, or torturing of combatants are the most upset. Repeated exposure to such atrocities shakes people to their moral core. They doubt the basic goodness of humans, including themselves. They wonder if God is still looking kindly upon their soul.

Increasingly, the professionals who work with veterans are coming to believe that the concept of moral injury is more useful than the standard psychiatric diagnosis of PTSD in providing a construct for understanding the unique difficulties faced by returning veterans. Psychologist Kent D. Drescher, who works at the National Center for PTSD in Palo Alto, California, summarizes the symptoms and difficulties associated with moral injury as (1) negative changes in ethical attitudes, (2) changes in or loss of spirituality, (3) guilt, shame, and alienation, (4) anhedonia and dysphoria (mild depression, despair), (5) reduced trust in others and in social/cultural contracts, (6) aggressive behaviors, and (7) poor self-care or self-harm.[4] This list suggests that moral injury is a robust concept, a unique blending of psychological, social, spiritual, and moral factors. It also includes some serious or potentially serious symptoms. In recent years, authorities in the United States have become very concerned about the large number of veterans who take their own lives or act self-destructively through chemical addiction. Although there may be many reasons for suicide and addiction among the returning soldiers, moral injury may be a helpful lens through which to understand this disturbing trend.

Mediating Forgiveness

Guilt and shame are part of life. Human beings do make mistakes, either by commission or omission. Humans are fallible. People struggling with survivor's guilt or moral injury deeply need and want a sense of forgiveness. For moral and conscientious people, it is not enough to just dismiss such guilt as unfounded or as the product of a dysfunctional family. They need a path forward. Trying to find that path forward, many people will seek out the counsel of ministers, chaplains, and priests. Ministers do mediate forgiveness through prayers of confession, Scriptural assurances of forgiveness, rituals of reconciliation, and of course the sacrament of Communion or Eucharist. These ritual moments might occur in the immediate aftermath of trauma, in the subsequent months of bereavement and grief work, or toward the end of the recovery and healing process as a sign and celebration of a new inner peace. This process takes different forms in the various branches of Christianity, but confession and forgiveness are central.

4. Drescher and Foy, "When They Come Home," 92.

Forgiveness and the Future

Earlier, I suggested that a person with PTSD could be understood as someone who is trapped in the past. Indeed, dreams, flashbacks, retraumatizations, and reenactments all seem to be dynamics that are fixated on the past, on repeating the past, on reliving the past, and on keeping the person mentally in the past. I would suggest that revenge, particularly chronic vengeful attitudes and behaviors, functions the same way. People who are consumed with thoughts of revenge are similarly fixated on the past, on the offending hurt, injustice, or horror. In a sense, revenge is a way of reliving the trauma, and it sometimes leads to a literal reenactment of the trauma. Revenge is a way of keeping the trauma alive, extending its impact well into the future, even onto the next generation. In contrast, I would suggest that forgiveness could be understood as a way of letting go of the past, becoming at peace with the past, releasing oneself to live more fully in the present. "Without forgiveness there really is no future," writes Archbishop Desmond Tutu, 1984 Nobel Peace Prize laureate.[5] Tutu was referring to his nation, South Africa, which was emerging from the collective trauma of apartheid, and the work of the Truth and Reconciliation Commission that he chaired. His words, however, are equally applicable to individuals. Forgiveness, if appropriately done, frees people from the past and allows a new future. Some religious groups even believe that forgiveness frees the soul of the deceased person to move on to the next life, in contrast to revenge, which keeps everyone stuck in the past.

Recovering from trauma or traumatic loss, especially if another human being caused it, is very difficult. The way of forgiveness may not be for everyone. It is clearly the narrow highway, the road less traveled. It is hard work. My primary point here is that it is one of the pathways for drawing close to God and enriching one's spiritual life.

Embracing Gratitude

When people are asked how they have managed to survive or even grow through a significant trauma or traumatic loss event, they usually are quite humble. Many report that they do not do it on their own. They are quick to say that they could not have done it without human support and without divine intervention. They cite little moments of strength amid the pain,

---

5. Tutu, *No Future Without Forgiveness*, 255.

moments of mystical coincidence, key moments when a friend showed up or said the right thing. For all of these moments of grace, they are grateful. In short, growth is experienced as a gift.

Robert A. Emmons, a psychologist who has focused on the scientific study of gratitude, writes that gratitude includes two elements. One is "the *acknowledgment* of goodness in one's life. In gratitude we say yes to life." And, "Gratitude is *recognizing* that the source(s) of this goodness lie at least partially outside the self."[6] But, trauma or traumatic loss can challenge a person's basic assumption about the goodness of life.

At first blush, it might appear that trauma and gratitude do not go together. Significant losses and traumas have a way of bringing people to their knees. The illusion of self-sufficiency is shattered along with that of self-importance. People are humbled. In being humbled, they become more open, more open to asking for help from God and from others, more open to experiencing God's compassion and mercy. And if they receive an unexpected miracle or deliverance and/or receive human support or generosity, they are grateful, even brought to tears. In the framework of Emmons, they both acknowledge the goodness in their lives (gratitude), however limited, and recognize that its source is outside of themselves (humility). Indeed, the experience of trauma or traumatic loss can open the door to a profound experience of gratitude and humility.

Acknowledging gratitude can grow out of the radical reordering of values that sometimes accompanies trauma. In the aftermath of a significant loss or trauma, all of the things (e.g., possessions, status, appearance) that seemed so important prior to the loss or trauma are now seen as trifling. Often, a tornado survivor says, "It is all just things, and things can be replaced. I am just thankful we are all alive." A grieving daughter says, "I am just thankful that Mom did not suffer." Or a cancer patient states, "I am just glad they caught it in time." All of the people and blessings that trauma survivors had taken for granted even just a few days earlier are now very much appreciated. Similarly, natural disasters have a way of leveling the playing field, at least temporarily. In a collective trauma, there are no rich and poor, no racial distinctions . . . everyone is in the same boat together. Natural disasters often create or strengthen community. Natural disasters and similar traumatic losses have a way of humbling people and triggering moments of gratitude.

6. Emmons, *Thanks!*, 4.

Gratitude is not easy. It is not the automatic or typically the first response to a traumatic death, especially when there was no miracle or last-minute escape. Traumatic death throws most people into intense suffering, into feelings of anger, self-pity, sorrow, guilt, and intense pain. "Suffering robs us of easy gratitude," writes Emmons. "In fact, the road to recovery is one in which we must fight a hard battle to regain the ability to appreciate the good things we still enjoy, to banish anger, sullen ingratitude and depression, and to regain the ability to enjoy our lives."[7] People in the midst of suffering can appreciate acutely the small mercies of life. Gratitude and grace can be present in latent forms, even in the early and intense stages of trauma recovery and grief work, if one has the eyes to see them.

Gratitude as a Sign of Healing

Joe Biden was vice president of the United States from 2009 to 2017. His oldest son, Beau, died of brain cancer in the prime of life in May 2015, a tragedy compounded by the earlier death of Beau's mother in an auto accident in 1972. When Biden was considering entering the campaign for the Democratic nomination for president later that year, he said: "There will come a time when the memory of Beau will bring a smile to our lips, instead of a tear to our eyes . . . but we are not there yet."[8]

Biden's sense was that he and his family were not yet ready to make a new emotional investment because their grief work was not over. Interestingly, his words imply that the emergence of gratitude is one of the signs that would indicate that their grief process was complete. If the grief process does its work, gratitude gradually pushes out sorrow, anger, self-pity, and depression. It takes a while, sometimes years, but if all goes well, gratitude prevails. The emergence of gratitude is a sure sign that grief has done its work.

Gratitude usually emerges more fully toward the end of a successful grief process. Gratitude normally takes some time. In a sense, gratitude might be understood as the goal of the grief process. Healing might be understood as a shift from "tears to smiles," a shift in focus from what one

7. Emmons, *Thanks!*, 156.

8. White House Press Conference, October 25, 2015, https://www.bustle.com/articles/118500-transcript-of-joe-bidens-speech-reads-just-like-announcment-speech-aside-from-well-you-know.

does not have now to what one did have, a shift from resentment to gratitude and maybe even from sorrow to joy. Yet, as I implied above, gratitude can also be experienced concurrently with the emotional work of recovery and grief as little moments of grace, relief, even humor amid the larger suffering. People might be thankful for a friend's unexpected support, for the miracles of modern medicine, for sleeping through the night without a nightmare, for moments of beauty amid the ugliness of a battlefield. In other words, gratitude might also be understood not just as the goal of the healing process but as a perspective that enhances and facilitates the healing process.

Even in the immediate aftermath of trauma, some people remark, "It could have been worse." I have wondered about this kind of comment. Is it denial? Is it a type of dark humor? Is it a way of comforting oneself? I am not a social scientist, but I have wondered if the people who come through great trauma with their faith intact are those who can claim an attitude of gratitude, however small or partial. Expressions of gratitude in the midst of trauma or trauma recovery have an "in spite of" quality—in spite of the suffering, "I am grateful that things were not worse." This is being grateful for what one can be grateful for without discounting in any way the tragedy of the moment. Such statements, however primitive, are statements of faith, statements of faith made in times of trauma. As such, they are empowering.

Serene Jones, in her book *Trauma and Grace: Theology in a Ruptured World*, makes the point that, among other things, trauma damages the human imagination. It "ruptures" and "disorders" the imagination of people caught in trauma.[9] It is hard for some traumatized persons to see God's presence and grace in the trauma event, and therefore it is difficult for them to feel grateful. Experiencing God's grace in the midst of trauma requires that one has eyes to see it, that one has an intact imagination. My hunch is that people who can see moments of grace in the middle of tragedy and people who can say, however simply or naively, that "things could have been worse" are more likely to survive and even grow spiritually in times of adversity. The challenge, then, for caregivers is to identify how to help people restore or heal their imaginative mechanisms so they can see the God who draws near to the wounded heart.

Gratitude cannot be forced, commanded, or prescribed. If ministers try to make gratitude a "should" or preach gratitude too early in the recovery and grief process, they will do more harm than good. They will be

---

9. Jones, *Trauma and Grace*, 20.

perceived as insensitive and will be fostering denial. Gratitude, whether as the result of healing or as a perspective on life, has to emerge on its own, born in the pain of sorrow. Ministers can only plant the seeds of gratitude. Ultimately, gratitude is a gift. It is a miracle, a small miracle that fosters spiritual growth in and through significant loss events. When those seeds begin to grow and a grateful heart emerges, ministers should encourage people to say "thank you." Taking time, even while still in the midst of recovery and/or bereavement, to give thanks to those who have helped, to a benevolent God, is good for the soul. Expressions of gratitude facilitate the recovery and healing process.

Rituals of Gratitude

In my area of the country, funerals and memorial services are increasingly being called or subtitled celebrations of life. Clearly, the ethos of grief rituals is shifting away from sorrow and grief and toward celebration and gratitude. Most celebrations include one or more eulogies for the deceased. Eulogies tend to focus mourners on the positive, on what people appreciated or admired about the deceased or found to be thankful about the deceased's life. He or she may have been a scoundrel but, in the ritualized moment, loved ones can usually find positive things to say about the departed. People might even laugh a bit as they recall an endearing trait or amusing story of the departed. What is said or how truthful the eulogy is matters little. The pain and disappointment do not go away, but good eulogies make people both cry and laugh, and in the moments of laughter there are gratitude and grace. Healing requires both tears and laughter.

Recovering or grieving people may also look for ways to express their gratitude informally. They might want to give a financial gift to the church to give thanks to God. They might want to make a financial gift to the hospice or the hospital that cared for their loved one in his or her last days. They might want to establish a memorial or a foundation as a way of giving back. They might find it helpful to write a thank you letter to the health care professionals who cared for and comforted them in their time of loss. They might even want to say thank you in person to the first responders who acted so bravely on their behalf. All of these gestures and many more need to be understood as a natural part of or the culmination of the healing process. They both facilitate healing and are at times a sign of its completion.

Spirituality

Ministers are accustomed to responding to people in crisis, in grief, and in the midst of tragedy, but ministers and other caregivers should be equally perceptive of the potential moments of celebration and thanksgiving that might surface toward the end of the recovering and grieving process. As people experience healing and recovery, in mind, body, and/or spirit, this goodness can be ritualized and celebrated. This might take the form of a ritual that marks a new identity, a new story, a transformed life narrative, a new love, a new stage of life, a restoration of health, or a reconciliation between people. Ritualizing and marking the positive moments are as important as ritualizing the moments of agony, loss, and heartache. Joy can also be an important part of the journey toward wholeness.

Reshaping the Narrative of Your Life

In chapters 2 and 4, I summarized three types of stories that emerge in trauma recovery and grief work. I characterized the three types of stories as stories about *how*, *what*, and *who*. The *how* are the trauma stories; the *what* include grief stories about what was lost; and the *who* include survival stories or growth stories. In this chapter, I have explored three ways that people can grow spiritually in and through trauma recovery and grief work that also shaped and reshape the stories people tell of their trauma, recovery, and healing. Yet, there is one more piece of narrative work to do. The final piece of the work is to integrate these stories into one's life narrative.

In this book, I have tried to describe a journey, a journey from trauma to recovery to grief work and to spiritual growth. Not everyone completes this journey. Most complete some of the journey. Others are on the journey for years and years. One of the signs that people are in the final stages of this work are the questions they ask. What continuing role will this trauma play in my life? How important will this trauma event be in the long run? Will this trauma define me or will I define myself by something larger than this tragedy? How does this trauma fit into God's plan for my life? How has my life story changed in light of this experience? How will I remember—how will I tell the story of this phase of my life journey? Ministers and other spiritual caregivers can be helpful by listening for these questions, lifting them up, and supporting folks as they story afresh.

In answering these questions, people reshape or edit their life narrative, now taking into account the whole experience, the tragedy and the pain but also the growth and the deepened spirituality. How they change or edit the narrative of their lives depends on how well they have done their recovery and grief work and even their soul work described in this chapter. If the recovery and healing have not gone well or remain unfinished, people tend to be unable to answer the above questions or answer them with partial, negative, or distorted answers. They continue to define themselves and limit themselves by their trauma. Their trauma story continues to be *the* story of their lives.

On the other hand, if the recovery and healing processes have gone reasonably well, then the trauma is no longer the defining life event. It becomes just a part of the individual's continuing life journey. "I am larger than this trauma," said one recovering woman, adding, "I will not be defined by this tragedy!" In the midst of trauma recovery, claiming to be a "survivor" was empowering. Now that label seems limiting. Her real identity is rooted in her larger life narrative, in her journey of faith. Such people have integrated their loss or trauma event into a larger and now more complex and richer life narrative. In this way, they have not just recovered, survived, or even grown. They have overcome.

Questions for Personal Reflection

1. How do you define spirituality? How is it different from or related to your theology? What do you do to nurture your spirituality?

2. How do you resolve the theodicy dilemma? How many different Christian or biblical responses can you give to this quandary?

3. Do you find evil to be a useful concept as a descriptive term in the context of trauma? Are some things or people just plain evil?

4. Find a copy online of the Pargament's Religious Coping Activities Scale (RCOPE) (www.faith-health.org/?P=158&lang=en). Take it to see which coping style you prefer.

5. What has been the most challenging person or situation for you to forgive? How did you do it? Are you satisfied with the results?

6. Do you hold a grudge? How does that grudge function in your spiritual walk?

7. Do Christians have the right and freedom to not forgive?

8. How are funeral and memorial services changing in your area of the country or subculture? What are the pros and cons of the increasing emphasis on "celebration" as a description of a funeral or memorial service?
9. Keep a gratitude journal for a week and report on your experiences. Gratitude journals are described in *Thanks!* by Emmons.
10. Do you define yourself by the traumas in your life? How does your spiritual identity help you not overidentify with the traumas and losses in your life?

7

Theological Postscript

THE ARREST, TRIAL, AND execution of Jesus of Nazareth was a trauma, certainly for his followers and maybe even for Jesus. In spite of Jesus' hints as to what was coming, for his disciples his arrest appears to have been unexpected. It was a shock, especially because Jesus seemed to allow it, resisted fighting back, and quietly accepted his fate. The disciples fled for their lives! Surely, they might have been arrested and executed too. To be even seen as one of his followers, to be recognized by their Galilean accent, might have cost them their lives. Next the mock trial took place, which was again shocking in that Jesus was mute. Then, he was dragged through the city streets, when only a few days earlier he had ridden through those streets as a king coming to his coronation. Then, the crucifixion occurred. The women watched his agony. They prayed for a last-minute miracle, for the heavens to open up and an army of angels to descend. The death of Jesus was a trauma because it was unexpected; it was horrific; it was life-threatening; and it was emotionally overwhelming. It met all of the criteria for trauma.

If this is true, what is the significance of Christianity being born in trauma? What does it mean to Christians today that trauma is at the heart of our faith?

As with all significant traumas, the death of Jesus created a crisis of meaning among his followers. Their foundations were shaken. Was he really the Messiah? This was not what we expected the Messiah to do. How could God allow this to happen to such a good man? How do we make sense of this? The resurrection initially created more confusion. Is Jesus

Theological Postscript

alive or dead? Will the promised kingdom come now? Where are the avenging angels?

The crisis of meaning was resolved by Jesus' followers, perhaps inspired by the risen Lord, with the conviction that this was not a senseless tragedy but that Jesus is the Messiah (Luke 24:13–35) and the Lamb of God who takes away the sins of the world. After all, it happened on Passover. It was all planned. Seeing the trauma in this positive light transformed Golgotha into "good" Friday. It was no longer a trauma but something positive, glorious; the crucifixion had been transformed from a meaningless tragedy to the salvation of the world. This is one of the greatest "reframes" in the history of human civilization.

This understanding of the trauma of Jesus' execution is embodied in the story of the Last Supper. Jesus willingly gives up his body and blood to secure divine forgiveness for sinners. His suffering has a purpose. He is our Savior. He is the agent of our salvation, but in order to be our Savior in this frame of reference, Jesus had to become sinless, more like the Son of God than the Son of Man. The Apostle Paul embraces and promotes this interpretation of the trauma. He solidifies and explains it theologically. It makes sense to him partly because he operated in a Jewish legal and philosophical framework. And this meaning of the trauma of the cross still makes sense today, especially for people trying to be perfect or even trying to be good enough by some external measure.

An alternative, perhaps the original, understanding of how humanity is saved focuses more on Easter than on Good Friday. We are saved because in the resurrection God conquers death and thereby releases humanity from its bondage to fear, a bondage imposed upon us by Satan and intensified by trauma, injustice, and evil. There is no need to sugarcoat the crucifixion by positing that it was preplanned. Jesus' execution was a tragedy. It was traumatic and evil. We are saved not by the cross but by the resurrection. We are saved because God reveals that trauma and death are not the final word, that the gates of heaven are open, that there is eternal life in Christ's Way. God could not stop the trauma of Golgotha, but God can transform trauma. In a sense, God is our savior, not Jesus Christ. Easter is God's miracle, God's doing (Jesus may have been as surprised as anyone by his resurrection). And if nothing else, Pentecost is the empowerment phase of trauma recovery, a transformation of fearful disciples into courageous apostles.

This interpretation of the trauma of Holy Week posits that God was present with Jesus in his suffering and thereby transcended the trauma. It offers a different vision of the divine, not as a lawgiver sitting on a throne above humanity's struggles, requiring that divine justice be satisfied with a sacrifice, but as an active creative participant in humanity's sufferings. God is not the cause of trauma but the redeemer of trauma.

This message speaks to the deepest need of humanity, which is release from our bondage to fear. This message assumes that humanity's original sin is not our disobedience and estrangement from God but our fear. Fear turns us away from life, from love, from God, and from joy. Fear corrupts us and is at the root of our violence and cruelty. The primary existential issue of humanity is not "Am I good enough?" but "How do we overcome our innate fear?" Our fear is that we shall die, and do so alone and without meaning.

For people for whom the primary existential issue is "Am I good enough?" the Pauline interpretation of the trauma of Jesus' death still has great appeal. But I would suggest that in the twenty-first century, in this emerging post-Christian, postmodern world, there is a growing number of people for whom the primary existential challenge is not how to be good enough but how to transcend trauma.

What does it mean to Christians in the twenty-first century that trauma is at the heart of our faith? How should Christians understand and proclaim the good news of the death and resurrection of Jesus in the twenty-first century?

Over the course of Christian history, I believe, Christianity has had a special appeal to those who have been traumatized or oppressed or have suffered unjustly. This is precisely because the message that God was in the midst of trauma, comforting the victims and transforming their suffering into a greater good, is a powerful message.

Over the years, Christianity has become institutionalized, become a religion of the establishment as well as of the downtrodden. People of wealth and power also experience trauma, of course, but Christianity loses its power if it becomes too closely aligned with the sinners instead of aligning with those who are sinned against. If Christianity wants to renew itself, it needs to focus on what it has historically done, which is to be in ministry to and with the traumatized of the world. Christianity is, after all, a faith born in trauma.

THEOLOGICAL POSTSCRIPT
Questions for Personal Reflection

1. Do a critical Bible study that explores the following question textually: Was the execution of Jesus preplanned or was it a unexpected trauma?
2. What does it mean to you personally, to your salvation, that trauma is at the heart of Christianity?
3. The author presents, however briefly, two views of how we are saved. Which view do you resonate with and why? Are they mutually exclusive? Does one view or the other seem to resonate with different generational groups in your congregation?

Appendix 1

Discussion Questions and Activities for Classroom Use

Introduction

1. What questions or needs do you bring with you to the reading of this book (or to your class or training program as a whole) concerning loss, grief, and trauma?

Chapter 1: Trauma

1. This chapter offers four vignettes of different kinds of trauma. Go online and research the incidence of trauma events in the United States. For example, how many Americans experience a natural disaster in their lifetime? How many Americans will be a victim of a crime in their lifetime?
2. Many current movies are about trauma in one form or another. Find a movie that deals with trauma and portrays a character with PTSD. How do you understand the character's struggle in terms of the features of PTSD?
3. Find a treatment program in your community for people suffering from PTSD related to war. Find a treatment program for people

Appendix 1

suffering from being raped or sexually assaulted. Many of these professionals would be glad to speak to your class, if invited.

4. Does it help to give people who are suffering a diagnostic label? How does it help? How does it not help? Why?
5. Interview a hospital or military chaplain. What are the kinds of traumas that chaplains routinely encounter?
6. Do you think that people overuse the words *trauma, traumatic,* and *PTSD* these days? If so, why is that? What are the benefits and drawbacks of using these terms?
7. Go online and read about the Adverse Childhood Events Study. Share what you learned with a friend or classmates. What are the typical signs of childhood trauma?
8. Do you think that trauma symptoms can be passed down from generation to generation?
9. Sometimes we cry because we are sad, and sometimes we cry because we are overwhelmed. How do the symptoms of trauma compare to the symptoms typically associated with loss? Discuss this distinction in light of trauma recovery work and grief support work.
10. Research the history of trauma studies and PTSD in the United States over the last hundred years. How does the way we understand trauma shape culture, and how is trauma shaped by culture?

Chapter 2: Recovery

1. The word *recovery* is used in both trauma work and addictions work. What are the parallels between trauma and addiction and the interface between the two?
2. From the beginning, Christians have been telling stories of Jesus, stories of faith. How have we struggled with the imperative to "get the story right"?
3. Many times, chaplains or ministers are called upon to accompany military or medical personnel who are notifying the next of kin of a traumatic death of their loved one. Interview a chaplain about the guidelines for death notification work. How do they perform that task with compassion and informed professionalism?

Discussion Questions

4. Do online research on the impact of trauma upon the human brain and nervous system. What metaphor best describes what happens to the brain in trauma? What is the essential information caregivers need to know about neuroscience in this regard?
5. Who are the therapists or agencies in your community who are trained to provide services for trauma victims? How do you evaluate or choose a therapist?
6. What do you think of Junger's contention that the PTSD associated with veterans has as much to do with their reentry into civilian society as it does with their battlefield experiences?
7. Research online the response of the Amish community to the 2006 shooting at one of their schools in Lancaster County, Pennsylvania, that took the lives of eight children. How do you evaluate their response theologically, ethically, and in terms of trauma recovery?
8. Spiritual directors are Christian guides to various spiritual practices. If you are in seminary, take a class in spiritual direction or find your own spiritual director. If you are in ministry, find a spiritual director you can meet with regularly.
9. In what ways does the Serenity Prayer speak to or help people in trauma recovery or doing significant grief work?
10. One of the earliest pioneers in the use of meditation to reduce stress was Jon Kabat-Zinn. His approach is called Mindfulness-Based Stress Reduction. Online, research his approach by viewing or listening to one of his lectures.

Chapter 3: Loss

1. List as many examples of secondary losses, collective losses, chronic losses, disenfranchised losses, and developmental losses as you can.
2. How does the experience of collective loss or collective trauma shape the identity and psychological makeup of people, even those several generations removed from the tragedy?
3. If you are currently a minister, maybe you have been called upon to lead a collective ritual, such as a memorial service for the victims of a disaster in your town, a national prayer breakfast on the anniversary

APPENDIX 1

of 9/11, or an ecumenical prayer service after three nights of violence over a police shooting. How did you do?

4. Do you think that the impact of a loss depends not just on *what is lost* and *how it is lost* but also on the age of the person experiencing the loss? Why or why not?
5. How do you respond to the idea that the death of a child is the loss of the future; the death of a spouse is the loss of the present; and the death of parent(s) is the loss of the past?
6. Interview a classmate or colleague who is an immigrant. How did they experience the losses and gains associated with immigration, and how did the church help them navigate that transition?
7. How is change understood in evolutionary theory?
8. Watch the Disney movie *Inside Out*. How do these characters illustrate the dynamics of transition, loss, and change?
9. How do we help people see the hidden gains in loss events without reinforcing denial?
10. Draw five concentric circles. Place in the innermost circle those people most cherished by you and then fill in each of the remaining circles with the names of other people you care about, with those of least importance to you in the outermost circle. Now add a wide range of entities that you value to each of the circles: places, pets, personal abilities and skills, possessions, ideas, etc. How does this graphic reflect your potential for loss? How does it represent your values profile?

Chapter 4: Grief

1. Go online and research the rate of recovery among bereaved adults. According to behavioral scientists, what percentage of adults recover from a significant loss and how long does it take?
2. Using English dictionaries and similar resources, clarify the distinctions between empathy, sympathy, and compassion. What insights about caregiving surface from this research?
3. In the classic *Star Wars* movies, what is the origin of evil? What causes Anakin Skywalker to turn to the dark side? Wasn't it unresolved grief?

Discussion Questions

Can you think of other movies or stories in which unresolved grief leads to evil?

4. Research the meaning of despair, especially in theological literature. How is despair different from or similar to depression? How would a minister care for a congregant who is depressed vs. one who is despairing?
5. Have you participated in a spontaneous collective ritual? What was it, and what was it like for you? What need did it fulfill in you?
6. How have the rituals and ritualization associated with loss, grief, and life transitions changed or stayed the same over the last hundred years in the United States?
7. The biggest collective trauma in the lives of the ancient Israelites was the destruction of Jerusalem in the fifth century BCE. The book of Lamentations arose out of that trauma. What can you learn about how the laments in Lamentations were actually used in rituals?
8. Go online to https://complicatedgrief.columbia.edu to learn about a specialized treatment program for people struggling with complicated bereavement. What are the signs and symptoms of complicated bereavement?
9. If clergy need to be ritual artists in the twenty-first century, not just ritual leaders, what new skills do they need to learn or how should seminary curricula be adapted to meet this vision?
10. Go online and research the incidence of compassion fatigue in various professions, including clergy. Do similar research for the term *clergy burnout*. What programs does your denomination have to prevent burnout or treat ministers who are experiencing compassion fatigue or burnout?

Chapter 5: Growth

1. Describe ways in which you have grown as a result of a significant loss or traumatic event.
2. Go online and find a copy of the Posttraumatic Growth Inventory. Take the inventory yourself. Try it out on your friends. Is it a useful tool?

Appendix 1

3. Research the phrase *ministry of empowerment.* What kinds of ministries are Christians engaged in under that rubric?

4. Go online and research the concept of Stockholm syndrome. How should we understand this dynamic in light of trauma theory?

5. A common adage among the bereaved is that it is not wise to make big decisions in the early stages of bereavement. Trauma has a way of stirring things up, almost demanding change. Is this adage applicable to trauma too? Why or why not?

6. Go online and find a copy of the World Assumptions Scale, which is a measuring device that grew out of Janoff-Bulman's book *Shattered Assumptions.* Take the test yourself and discuss its usefulness and accuracy in light of Christian theology.

7. If you were the minister responding to Joel in the vignette in this chapter, how would you help this young man? What do you see as the issues and concerns in the vignette? What caregiving strategies seem appropriate?

8. The most significant natural disaster in the Bible is the flood (Gen 7). The Genesis story of the flood and Noah parallels similar accounts in Babylonian literature, but how is the Genesis story different from other versions? How did this "difference" help the Hebrews make sense of this senseless event?

9. Look up the American Psychological Association's 2014 essay "The Road to Resilience" (http://www.apa.org/helpcenter/road-resilience.aspx). What does this material tell you about the factors that help people survive and perhaps grow through loss or trauma? How does this list compare to traditional Christian virtues?

10. Discuss the author's suggestion at the end of this chapter that a good mission for the church in the twenty-first century might to build resilience through character formation.

Chapter 6: Spirituality

1. How do you define spirituality? What do you make of the growing number of people who say they are "spiritual but not religious"? Is this an example of the rise in interest in spirituality or is it an example of the decline of organized religion?

Discussion Questions

2. Research the traditional ways that Christian theologians have resolved the theodicy problem. Does trauma trump or scramble these traditional answers?
3. The Christian view of God includes the idea of a just God. Find a Christian hymn or biblical passage that seems to blur the line between God seeking justice and God seeking revenge.
4. Go online and research the concept of self-compassion. How does self-compassion relate to a God of compassion?
5. Is violence a male problem? Is revenge the male way of avoiding grief?
6. Go online and research restorative justice. What is it? Where is it being put into practice in your area? Interview a leader or facilitator of restorative justice. How does it mitigate the effects of trauma?
7. Watch *The Power of Forgiveness*, a 2008 film directed by Martin Doblmeier. Much of the video presents forgiveness in the context of trauma. It will spark reflection and discussion regarding the efficacy of forgiveness.
8. Go to the website of Brite Divinity School's Soul Repair Center. Find out about their work and report back to your class or colleagues.
9. Are there some types of offenses that should not be forgiven and should not be forgotten? How do people forgive but not forget?
10. What would be your pastoral approach if you were the minister in the vignette about Heather? How would you blend psychological theory and Christian spirituality?

Theological Postscript

1. What is the significance of trauma's location at the heart of the Christian faith? What are the implications for the future of Christianity?

Bibliography

Alexander, Jeff. *Trauma: A Social Theory.* New York: Polity, 2012.
American Psychiatric Association. *Diagnostic and Statistical Manual of Mental Disorders (DSM-5).* 5th ed. Washington, DC: American Psychiatric Association, 2013.
Anderson, Herbert, and Edward Foley. *Mighty Stories, Dangerous Rituals: Weaving Together the Human and Divine.* San Francisco: Jossey-Bass, 1998.
Bass, Ellen, and Laura Davis. *The Courage to Heal: A Guide for Women Survivors of Child Sexual Abuse.* 4th ed. New York: Collins Living, 2008.
Becker, Ernest. *Denial of Death.* New York: Free, 1973.
Becvar, Dorothy S. *In the Presence of Grief: Helping Family Members Resolve Death, Dying, and Bereavement Issues.* New York: Guilford, 2001.
Boss, Pauline. *Ambiguous Losses: Learning to Live with Unresolved Grief.* Cambridge, MA: Harvard University Press, 2000.
Breazeale, Kathlyn A. *Mutual Empowerment: A Theology of Marriage, Intimacy, and Redemption.* Minneapolis: Fortress, 2008.
Briere, John, and Catherine Scott. *Principles of Trauma Therapy: A Guide to Symptoms, Evaluation and Treatment.* Thousand Oaks, CA: Sage, 2006.
Brock, Rita Nakashima, and Gabriella Lettini. *Soul Repair: Recovering from Moral Injury after War.* Boston: Beacon, 2012.
Brooks, David. *The Road to Character.* New York: Random House, 2015.
Brueggemann, Walter. Foreword to Ann Weems, *Psalms of Lament,* ix–xvii. Louisville: Westminster John Knox, 1995.
Burgess, Ann Wolbert, and Lynda Lytle Holmstrom. "Rape Trauma Syndrome." *American Journal of Psychiatry* 131, no. 9 (1974) 981–86.
Calhoun, Lawrence G., and Richard G. Tedeschi, eds. *The Handbook of Posttraumatic Growth: Research and Practice.* New York: Psychology, 2006.
Cole, Allan Hugh, Jr. *Be Not Anxious: Pastoral Care of Disquieted Souls.* Grand Rapids: Eerdmans, 2008.
Doehring, Carrie. *The Practice of Pastoral Care: A Postmodern Approach.* Louisville: Westminster John Knox, 2006.
Doka, Kenneth J. *Disenfranchised Grief: Recognizing Hidden Sorrow.* Lexington, MA: Lexington, 1989.
Drescher, Kent D., and David W. Foy. "When They Come Home: Posttraumatic Stress, Moral Injury, and Spiritual Consequences for Veterans." *Reflective Practice: Formation and Supervision in Ministry* 28 (2008) 85–102.

Bibliography

Ekman, Paul, and Wallace V. Friesen. *Unmasking the Face: A Guide to Recognizing Emotions from Facial Expressions.* Cambridge, MA: Malor, 2003.

Emmons, Robert A. *Thanks! How the New Science of Gratitude Can Make You Happier.* New York: Houghton Mifflin, 2007.

Erikson, Erik H. *Childhood and Society.* 2nd ed. New York: Norton, 1963.

Figley, Charles R., ed. *Compassion Fatigue: Coping with Secondary Traumatic Stress Disorder in Those Who Treat the Traumatized.* New York: Routledge, 1995.

Graham, Larry. *Moral Injury: Restoring Wounded Souls.* Nashville, TN: Abingdon, 2017.

Herman, Judith L. *Trauma and Recovery: The Aftermath of Violence—From Domestic Violence to Political Terror.* New York: Basic, 1992.

Hunsinger, Deborah van Deusen. *Bearing the Unbearable: Trauma, Gospel, and Pastoral Care.* Grand Rapids: Eerdmans, 2015.

Janoff-Bulman, Ronnie. *Shattered Assumptions: Towards a New Psychology of Trauma.* New York: Free, 1992.

Jones, Serene. *Trauma and Grace: Theology in a Ruptured World.* Louisville: Westminster John Knox, 2009.

Jordan, Alexander H., and Brett T. Litz. "Prolonged Grief Disorder: Diagnostic, Assessment, and Treatment Considerations." *Professional Psychology: Research and Practice* 45, no. 3 (2014) 180–87.

Junger, Sebastian. *Tribe: On Homecoming and Belonging.* New York: Twelve, 2016.

Kelley, Melissa M. *Grief: Contemporary Theory and the Practice of Ministry.* Minneapolis: Fortress, 2010.

Keshgegian, Flora A. *Redeeming Memories: A Theology of Healing and Transformation.* Nashville: Abingdon, 2000.

Klass, Dennis, et al., eds. *Continuing Bonds: New Understandings of Grief.* Philadelphia: Taylor and Francis, 1996.

Koenig, Harold G. *In the Wake of Disaster: Religious Responses to Terrorism and Catastrophe.* Philadelphia: Templeton, 2006.

Lewis, C. S. *A Grief Observed.* London: Faber and Faber, 1961.

Madigan, Stephen. *Narrative Therapy.* Theories of Psychotherapy Series. Washington, DC: American Psychological Association, 2010.

Means, J. Jeffrey. *Trauma and Evil: Healing the Wounded Soul.* Minneapolis: Fortress, 2000.

Mitchell, Kenneth R., and Herbert Anderson. *All Our Losses, All Our Griefs: Resources for Pastoral Care.* Philadelphia: Westminster, 1983.

Neimeyer, Robert A., ed. *Meaning Reconstruction and the Experience of Loss.* Washington, DC: American Psychological Association, 2001.

Neuger, Christie Cozad. *Counseling Women: A Narrative, Pastoral Approach.* Minneapolis: Fortress, 2001.

Nouwen, Henri J. M. *The Wounded Healer: Ministry in Contemporary Society.* New York: Image, 1979.

Pargament, Kenneth I. *The Psychology of Religion and Coping: Theory, Research, Practice.* New York: Guilford, 1997.

Park, Andrew Sung. *From Hurt to Healing: A Theology of the Wounded.* Nashville: Abingdon, 2004.

Parkes, Colin Murray. *Bereavement: Studies of Grief in Adult Life.* New York: International Universities, 1974.

———. *Love and Loss: The Roots of Grief and Its Complications.* New York: Routledge, 2006.

Bibliography

Rambo, Shelly. *Spirit and Trauma: A Theology of Remaining.* Louisville: Westminster John Knox, 2010.

Rogers, Dalene C. Fuller, and Harold G. Koenig. *Pastoral Care for Post-Traumatic Stress Disorder: Healing the Shattered Soul.* New York: Routledge, 2014.

Rynearson, Edward K. *Retelling Violent Death.* Philadelphia: Brunner-Routledge, 2001.

Scaer, Robert. *The Trauma Spectrum: Hidden Wounds and Human Resiliency.* New York: Norton, 2005.

Schiraldi, Glenn R. *The Post-Traumatic Stress Disorder Sourcebook: A Guide to Healing, Recovery, and Growth.* New York: McGraw-Hill, 1999.

Schwiebert, Pat, and Chuck DeKlyen. *Tear Soup: A Recipe for Healing after Loss.* Portland, OR: Grief Watch, 1999.

Seligman, Martin E. P. *Helplessness: On Development, Depression and Death.* San Francisco: W. H. Freeman, 1992.

Southwick, Steven M., and Dennis S. Charney. *Resilience: The Science of Mastering Life's Greatest Challenges.* New York: Cambridge University Press, 2012.

Taylor Shelley E., et al. "Biobehavioral Responses to Stress in Females: Tend-and-Befriend, Not Fight-or-Flight." *Psychological Review* 107, no. 3 (2000) 411–29.

Tutu, Desmond. *No Future Without Forgiveness.* New York: Image, 2000.

van der Kolk, Bessel. *The Body Keeps the Score: Brain, Mind, and Body in the Healing of Trauma.* New York: Penguin, 2014.

Volf, Miroslav. *The End of Memory: Remembering Rightly in a Violent World.* Grand Rapids: Eerdmans, 2006.

Westberg, Granger E. *Good Grief.* Minneapolis: Fortress, 2010.

Whitehead, James D., and Evelyn Eaton Whitehead. *The Virtue of Resilience.* Maryknoll, NY: Orbis, 2016.

Wimberly, Edward P., and Robert M. Franklin. *African American Pastoral Care and Counseling: The Politics of Oppression and Empowerment.* Cleveland, OH: Pilgrim, 2000.

Worden, Williams. *Grief Counseling and Grief Therapy: A Handbook for Mental Health Practitioners.* 4th ed. New York: Springer, 2009.

Wright, H. Norman. *The Complete Guide to Crisis and Trauma Counseling.* Minneapolis: Bethany House, 2011.

Zinner, Ellen S., and Mary Beth Williams. *When a Community Weeps: Case Studies in Group Survivorship.* Philadelphia: Brunner/Mazel, 1999.